the GOD
who I fell
from
HEAVEN

the GOD who fell from HEAVEN

by John Shea

THE THOMAS MORE PRESS
Chicago, Illinois

The God Who Fell from Heaven was originally published
in 1979 by Argus Communications (Niles, Illinois), a
division of DLM, Inc. (Allen, Texas).

Cover design by Jean Morman Unsworth

ISBN 0-88347-276-7

�✸✸✸✸✸✸✸✸✸✸✸✸✸✸✸✸✸✸✸✸✸✸✸✸

CONTENTS

✖✖✖✖✖✖✖✖✖✖✖✖✖✖✖✖✖✖✖✖✖✖✖✖✖✖

"Music and Laughter and Good Red Wine"

In the living room of Andrew's home there hangs a banner. It stretches from the ceiling to the floor and is as wide as five smiling children. In red and blue it reads:

> Where 'er the Catholic sun does shine
> There's music and laughter and good red wine.
> At least I've always found it so
> Benedicamus Domino!

Stuck in the corner of the mirror in John's bathroom is a card. Every morning when he shaves, his face looks back at him over the words on the card.

> Lord, make me an instrument of your
> peace; where there is hatred, let me sow
> love; where injury, pardon;
> where there is doubt, faith; where there
> is despair, hope; where there is darkness,
> light; and where there is sadness, joy.
>
> O, Divine Master, grant that I may
> not so much seek to be consoled as to
> console; to be understood, as to
> understand; to be loved as to love; for it is
> in giving that we receive, it is in pardoning
> that we are pardoned, and it is in
> dying that we are born to eternal life.

Above the sink in Alice's kitchen there is a shelf. It is uncluttered. "The only shelf in the house that is not a slum," she often says. On

✖✖✖✖✖✖✖✖✖✖✖✖✖✖✖✖✖✖✖✖✖✖✖✖✖✖

it is a slender glass vase with a single flower and a piece of decoupage wood on a simple wire tripod. Its wrinkled surface bears the words:

> *The air*
> *The mothering air, the hollows,*
> *nest of birds,*
> *these things remind me always*
> *of a God who holds us in herself*
> *as in a womb.*

Any individual prayer may be, at best, beautiful and poetic or, at worst, routine and uninspired. But the fascinating thing about prayers is where they turn up. The prayer that leaps from Andrew's wall is an introduction to the hospitable man who owns the home. The prayer that John must face in the morning is the prayer which, in muted and subtle ways, people hear from him all day long. And Alice is a woman who dwells within a nurturing God who is bringing her to birth. In other words, what is fascinating is not the prayer itself, but the way the prayer reflects the life experience of the one who prays. Prayers must never be stopped at but must be gone through to the experiences that have generated them. Prayers may be written down in books but their real home is the mouths of people.

"For all that has been — Thanks! To all that shall be — Yes!" is a beautiful prayer. It was written by Dag Hammarskjold and it reflects his life of praise, commitment, and courage. If we make that prayer our own, it is because it speaks to us. It picks up and expresses a conviction we feel and one which we want to deepen and make a guiding force in our lives. The first page of Nikos Kazantzakis's autobiography, *Report to Greco*, contains three prayers.

THREE KINDS OF SOULS, THREE PRAYERS:

1. I AM A BOW IN YOUR HANDS, LORD, DRAW ME, LEST I ROT.

2. DO NOT OVERDRAW ME, LORD, I SHALL BREAK.

3. OVERDRAW ME, LORD, AND WHO CARES IF I BREAK!

These prayers reflect the lifelong struggle of Kazantzakis to ride the harsh and demanding rhythms of the Mystery he found himself within. If we make his prayers ours, it is because we find in our lives a struggle similar to the one which gave rise to his words. Unless the prayers we speak are tightly linked to the lives we lead, they will be babbling we hide behind rather than true speech which reveals who we are in relation to All There Is.

Encounters

The aspect of life which individual prayers must reflect is the dimension of Mystery. As persons of prayer, we are sensitive that life is more than rocks, stars, and beetles. We are aware that we come and go within a More, a Whole, an Encompassing, a Presence. St. Paul's words resonate: "In God we live and move and have our being." The sensitivity is not the experience of God breaking into life from the outside but the experience of God breaking out of life from the inside. It is at first the suspicion and then the calm assurance that ordinary events reveal the extraordinary. Both the wrinkled skin of the newborn and the wrinkled skin of the aged are paths to the presence of God. Therefore, the goal of prayer is not to contact the missing God but to allow the present God to enter our minds and hearts.

Jesus knew this. Jesus was certainly, as current theology imagines him, a man for others. But he was also a scathing critic. One of his favorite targets was prayer. "In your prayer do not rattle on like the pagans. They think they will win a hearing by the sheer multiplication of words. Do not imitate them. Your Father knows what you need before you ask him." What Jesus is rebuking is the underlying image of God which forms the context of pagan prayer. Their God is pictured as an oriental potentate stretched lazily on a divan in the sky. He is inattentive and unknowing. Far removed from the struggles of the earth, he merely looks on with a mixture of disdain and amusement. Since this God is basically disinterested, the first move of the human person is to get his attention and the second is to hold it by constant chatter. The moment the words stop the fickleness of this God takes over and his head turns to other matters. Also since this God does not reside in the human heart, he is a stranger to human need. He clings to the divine prerogative of noninvolvement and so he must be informed about human pain and possibility.

Jesus' experience of God is the exact opposite of disinterest and distance, and therefore his prayer life is radically different. The image of Jesus' God is drawn from the prophetic tradition of Israel. This God does not know coolness. He alternately burns with love and anger. He is an insomniac who paces the night skies, his mind mulling over plans and his heart set on seducing the freedom of his sons and daughters. So urgent are his plots that he does not allow people to sleep. He visits their dreams and his opening line is always the same: "I have something for you to do." We do not need to attract the attention of this God for he is after us. And long prayers about our wishes will only drown out the sound of his voice with its single message about the kingdom of love and justice and peace. This God knows our secret drives and the back wards of our souls.

> *Yahweh, you examine me and you know me,*
> *you know if I am standing or sitting.*
> *The word is not even on my tongue,*
> *Yahweh, before you know the whole of it;*
> *close behind and close in front you fence me round,*
> *shielding me with your hand. (Psalm 139:1-3)*

For the pagans, God is distant and unconcerned and so prayer becomes an effort at contact and a plea for interest. For Jesus, God is both close and active and so prayer becomes the awareness of divine presence and the discernment of divine will.

THE GOD WHO FELL FROM HEAVEN

xxxxxxxxxxxxxxxxxxxxxxxxxxxxxx

Jesus' understanding of the God to whom he prays is reflected in the parables of the unjust judge and the friend at midnight. The common interpretation of these stories is that they are examples of perseverance in prayer. The judge does not give the widow her due at first, but because she is relentless in her request, he gives in. The friend does not gain entry into the house at first, but because he will not stop knocking, the householder finally opens the door and gives him the food he wishes. The point seems to be persistence. God is somewhat like an unjust judge and a sleepy householder, but our never-ceasing prayers will eventually turn him just and welcoming.

An alternate interpretation, leaning heavily on the prophetic tradition, identifies the cause of God with the widow and the friend outside and ourselves with the unjust judge and reluctant homeowner. This interpretation reverses out understanding of prayer. Prayer is not the verbal entreaty of a reluctant God but the way we relate and respond to a pursuing God. God is the widow, and if we will not give justice for the sake of justice, she will nag us till we give it out of embarrassment. God is the friend outside, and if we will not give bread out of friendship, he will knock till we give it out of annoyance. These parables are about prayer but they are not about how we should pray to God. They are about God's prayer for us — that we respond to his presence in the oppressed and the outcast.

In one tradition of the Old Testament the nearness of God is symbolized by what he owns. Human breath and blood belong to God. In the second account of creation God breathes into the nostrils of the man, his lungs fill, and life begins. The implication is that the inhalation of every person is the exhalation of God. Human life is sustained by divine breathing. Blood also belongs to God. When God searches out the murdering Cain, he does not confront him with the fact that he broke a sacred law. Instead he says, "Your brother's blood cries out to me from the ground." Whenever blood is spilled, the God of blood is summoned.

XXXXXXXXXXXXXXXXXXXXXXXXXXX

God is as close to human life as breath and blood. But this pervasive presence of God can paradoxically lead to a sense of his absence. For a reality so near can be easily taken for granted and overlooked. Since God is everywhere, the feeling can grow that he is nowhere. The difficulty of becoming aware of the rhythms of our breathing and the rushing of our blood reflects the difficulty of bringing into awareness the presence of the God who is as close as breath and blood.

Awareness of this pervasive presence of God to human life often occurs in "limit moments." When we crash and when we soar, the Mystery we dwell within often enters awareness. When the power of life surges through us and funds us, a prayer of praise arises. "O God, it's good to be alive!" But when the power of the Mystery ebbs and seems to abandon us, we find a prayer of petition in our throats. "God help me!" In moments of both hope and threat we become aware that we are inescapably related beyond ourselves.

In these times of the outbreak of the Mystery, the word God enters the human vocabulary. This word does not point to another tangible object of our experience but acknowledges a felt Presence. The most natural use of God language is not the nominative but the vocative case, not the way of naming but the way of addressing and exclaiming. The example of the skier brings the experiences of soaring and crashing and the use of God language together. The skier stands on the top of the mountain. He looks at the surrounding mountains which are stretched against the vast blueness of the Colorado sky. He exclaims, "O my God, how beautiful!" Then he looks down at the treacherous slope that twists below him. He exclaims a second time, "God, I could break my neck!" Mystery enters his awareness first through beauty and then through peril, and he acknowledges its presence by using the word *God*.

Another example is the story of the girl who was blind from birth. At the age of twenty she received the gift of eyes from a dying donor. After the operation, when the bandages were removed, she opened her eyes and quickly shut them. She was dazzled beyond her dreams.

THE GOD WHO FELL FROM HEAVEN

XXXXXXXXXXXXXXXXXXXXXXXXXX

Then she slowly opened them a second time and exclaimed, "O my God, how beautiful!" She did not see God; she saw the hospital room and bursts of color. This experience catapulted her into the awareness of the infinite Mystery she participates in, and so the word *God* emerged as a way of address and recognition.

Paradoxically, it is not only in experiences of wonder but also in experiences of horror that people find the word *God* in their mouths. In situations of great poverty or oppression the prayer arises, "O God, we have to do something about this!" or "O God, this cannot go on!" At these times Mystery enters into our awareness, but the impulse we receive from it is abhorrence. The Mystery and all who participate in it are shamed. The evil situation radically contradicts the nature of God, and so prayer in the presence of this God becomes a summons to change. The ways of the Mystery are myriad and the prayers of the Mystery dwellers are the responses of sensitive souls.

It should be noted that at these moments the Mystery seems to be "on the initiative" and we are in a situation of response. This feeling is the experiential basis for the ancient theological truth expressed by St. John: "God *first* loves us." The traditional definition of prayer is "a raising of the mind and heart to God." What is often not understood in that definition is who does the raising. In so many areas of our life we prize ourselves as self-starters; in our relationship to the Mystery we are responders. Our minds and hearts are raised at the instigation of the Insider God. To say "I will now pray" — or as leaders of public worship say, "Let us now pray" — is most appropriately translated as "Let us be open so that we may respond to the touch of God." Prayer is not an activity we engage in out of a determined will but something that happens as a result of the impact of the presence of God, which comes as a gift.

If the winter winds swing in from the northwest and the weather stays below freezing, a tundra forms along the shoreline of Lake Michigan. If you take the Outer Drive north from the Loop, you can see the rugged peaks of ice, frozen waves, extending into the lake. They are beautiful to look at but dangerous to walk on. They are

especially dangerous if you have recently lost two people you love and the day is the twenty-fourth of December. That is why Jim should never have been there. Today he says he isn't sure why he ventured onto the ice but he cannot forget what happened there. He remembers the tears, the loneliness, the hurt — and finally the peace arriving from nowhere and staying just long enough so the words "It's all right" were in perfect timing with his breath. It has been many years since that day, but in times of panic Jim remembers the words and peace returns like a promise that is always kept.

Reflections

Since prayer arises out of our encounters with the Mystery of life, praying is fundamentally the way we position ourselves within this Mystery. What we become immediately aware of in praying is that we are creatures. The acknowledgment and addressing of God is simultaneously the acknowledgment and addressing of ourselves as creatures. The presence of God reminds us that we are not God. The prayer of the Pharisee has forgotten this. "*I* give you thanks, O God, that *I* am not like the rest of men — grasping, crooked, adulterous. *I* thank you that *I* am not like the tax collector. *I* fast two days a week and *I* give you one-tenth of my income." God does not hear this prayer for, quite simply, it is not addressed to him. At the center of this prayer is the man himself. It is an exercise in narcissm. Creaturehood has been implicitly denied and God becomes a mere foil for the false glorification of the ego.

We never explicitly deny that we are creatures. The fact of limitation is so obvious that if we denied it, we would be laughed at. In an episode of "The Mary Tyler Moore Show" the death of a friend spurred the members of the news room to speculate on the arrangements of their own funerals. All began their plans with "When I die . . . " But when it came to Ted Baxter, he began with "If I die . . . " Ted Baxter is a character who carries all our human pretenses out in the open. He expresses what we feel but manage to hide. In this

XXXXXXXXXXXXXXXXXXXXXXXXXXXXX

incident he voices our misguided tendency to think that we are the indispensable center. The real reluctance on the part of many to pray may be rooted in the fact that prayer is a recognition that we are not self-sufficient. There is an element of dependency in our relationship with Mystery, and we often fear situations where we are not in total control. Yet the real function of this dependency is not to debilitate us but to free us from the burden of being perfect and encourage us in the task of being human. Our inescapable identity is that we are creatures, and our only consistent access to that identity is through genuine prayer. We pray lest we forget.

Fred is a businessman, successful and self-assured. Stuffed in his wallet among the many credit cards are two holy cards. One was passed out at his father's wake eight years ago; the other was available on the table near the Remembrance Book at his mother's wake just last year. On the back of the cards are traditional prayers for the dead with his parents' names inserted. He has scratched out the formal names and inserted "Mom" and "Dad." Fred says these prayers every day. When I ask why, he says he doesn't know. I ask if he thinks that by praying for his parents he thinks he will help them in the afterlife. He says no. He knows they are in the hands of God who is more merciful and inventive than his prayers. He says again he doesn't know but that when he says the prayers, he remembers his parents and knows who he is. He says it is a way of keeping his head straight. In the more abstract language of theology, Fred is bringing to mind his creaturehood and the God who sustains it.

To pray is to affirm implicitly but powerfully that we are not ultimate reality. But after this initial recognition (and it usually entails a shock), a further positioning goes on. From our final and inescapable identity as creatures we ask what is the meaning of various events and how we should relate to them. Our prayer becomes the way we appropriate the depth meanings of the situations we find ourselves in. Prayer centers us in the life stages from the perspective of the basic convictions of faith. In the celebrated parallels of Ecclesiastes there is a time for every season under the sun, a time to live and a time to die, a time for peace and a time for war, a time for planting and a time for uprooting. The implication is that if we live long enough, we will find ourselves in situations of panic and peace, of tears and laughter, of gathering and scattering. Prayer becomes the way we will occupy each of the seasons of our life. Prayer is not an effort to escape the inevitable and ambiguous rhythms of living but a way of participating in them. Through prayer we know who we are and how to dwell in moments of both dance and stillness.

Through prayer Jesus understood and related himself to the events of his life. The Gospels portray Jesus' prayer life as a natural companion of his ministry. He prayed before he chose the Twelve and before the cure of the epileptic boy. On two occasions in particular Jesus' prayer becomes an act of understanding and positioning. After an initial fascination with the message and ministry of Jesus, the powerful and influential among the Jewish people rejected him. The religious authorities, those seemingly in the best position to understand the revelation of God, not only walked away but actively plotted against him. In this situation Jesus prays, "Father, Lord of heaven and earth, to you I offer praise; for what you have revealed to the merest children." There could be many interpretations of this turn of events, but through his prayer Jesus seeks his Father's understanding of the situation and his will for it. The meaning that Jesus' prayer brings is that once again God is reversing expectations and choosing the lowly to bring about his Kingdom.

A second prayer of Jesus positions him with regard to his own death: "Father . . . take this cup away from me. But let it be as you would have it, not as I." Here is prayer in the hour of darkness. Jesus' first instincts are to avoid death, but through his prayer he attempts to uncover God's meaning for his death and to be faithful to it. Prayer is an act of our deepest selves through which we relate to the ongoing processes of life.

Jesus often began his teaching with, "If you have eyes to see and ears to hear . . ." Prayer can be understood as the cultivation of eyes that can see God's meaning and ears that can hear God's word. In both the Old and the New Testaments, the images of seeing and hearing are prominent. In the incidents of Moses at the burning bush and Peter at the empty tomb, three stages of seeing can be distinguished. At first Moses merely notices the fire on the mountainside. Then he turns aside "to go back and look at this strange sight." Finally, God is revealed and Moses' mission is given. At first, Peter casually glances into the tomb. Then he carefully scrutinizes it, and finally the truth of the resurrection is disclosed to him. Prayer is a process of sharpening our eyes so that glancing leads to scrutiny and scrutiny to revelation.

The image of hearing also unlocks the meaning of prayer. Solomon is wise because he did not ask for victory or honor or riches but for a "hearing heart," sensitive to the justice of God. The importance of ears that hear is succinctly stated by the psalmist:

> *Sacrifice and offering thou dost not desire;*
> *but thou has given me ears. (Psalm 40:6)*

Prayer is the way we see beyond the flat finish of life to its true depth, and the way we hear beyond the many words the one word that will save us.

Prayer that becomes penetrating sight and acute hearing must be a process of reflection. This means that, on the one hand, it cannot be unconnected with the ongoing events of life and that, on the other, it cannot be immersed in them. If we would pray, we have to get away. We need sacred places and sacred times to remind us of the holiness of every place and every time. The Gospels say that at key moments Jesus withdrew to mountainsides and gardens and deserts to pray. He needed a time and a place to reflect and to search out the intricate ways of God's Kingdom. "His reputation spread more and more, and great crowds gathered to hear him and to be cured of their maladies. He often retired to deserted places and prayed." Although prayers as a reflective process may not go on in those moments of life which William James called "booming, buzzing confusion," it is never far from personal problems and concrete possibilities. Prayer is not for its own sake as Jesus' warning reminds us: "None of those who cry out 'Lord, Lord,' will enter the kingdom of God but only the one who does the will of my Father in Heaven" (Matthew 7:21). Prayer may occur in solitude, but it reverberates in our interactions with each other.

Margaret found a "sack of pot" shoved way in the back of her fourteen-year-old son's sock drawer. She walked quickly from his room to the den where he was watching television and began to hit him. I met her on her way into church. She told me what happened and said, "I can't stand to look at him." She sat in the back of church with her thoughts and feelings and the God who at one and the same time hangs on the cross and lives in eucharistic bread of the tabernacle. On her way out I asked, "How's it going?"

"I prayed about it," she said.

"What did you find out?"

"He's not all bad and I'm not all good." She shrugged.

Prayer is what creatures do to their own lives before God.

Connections

The notion that prayer arises from an encounter with Mystery, and goes further to reflect through that Mystery on the events of personal life, can give the impression that prayer is an isolated endeavor, a purely individual project. In fact, prayer is often construed as the way we keep our individual relationship with God alive. Just as we cannot maintain friendship with someone we never talk to, so we cannot maintain friendship with God if we never converse with him. While this understanding is partially true, it can be seriously misleading. The God that Jesus proclaims does not cultivate exclusive, one-to-one relationships. For Jesus, to experience God is to experience his Kingdom, reconciliation among people. To call God Father is to experience other people as brothers and sisters. There is no way we can have a relationship with God independent of our relationships with each other. "The man who says he loves God but hates his neighbor is a liar." Prayer to the God of Jesus must broaden itself to include the neighbor.

This unbreakable relationship between God, the self, and the neighbor is reflected in the parable of the unmerciful servant. The servant sincerely thanks the master for forgiving his debt and his relationship with him is sound. But then the forgiven servant throttles a fellow servant with the demand, "Pay what thou owes!" When the master is informed, he is enraged and considers his own relationship with the servant sundered. The import of the story is that thanking God is not enough. The proper response to God is to imitate his mercy and love. To respond to God, as Jon Sobrino, a Latin American theologian, has suggested, is to correspond with him, to do his work in the world. Genuine prayer is not only the recognition of God and the acknowledgment of our status as creatures but also the expression of our bondedness to one another. The poet Anne Sexton says it simply: "To pray, Jesus knew/is to be a man carrying a man."

This binding together of God, self, and others is the fundamental dynamic of Jesus' central prayer, the "Our Father." The first two words, *our* and *Father*, already establish the connection. The divine reality we call Father is something we share between us. For Jesus a person could only say, "Our Father" if he had experienced God's love binding together the brothers and sisters. Yet two phrases later, the prayer asks: "Thy Kingdom come." The position of the one praying is between an initial experience of God's Kingdom and the petition that it be more fully experienced. The question arises, How does one grow in the experience of God, how does the Kingdom come more fully? The answer is cryptically given in the phrase "Forgive us our trespasses as we forgive those who have trespassed against us." The import of the phrase is not that if I forgive you then God will forgive me. This would merely be an even trade, a neat business transaction that any clever person would engage in. Nor is the meaning only that when we forgive each other, we mirror the

XXXXXXXXXXXXXXXXXXXXXXXXXX

forgiveness of God. At its deepest level the phrase suggests that *in the very act* of our forgiving each other we re-experience the forgiving love of God. The experience of God deepens only when it brings reconciliation, when it is shared with the brothers and the sisters. The connection between God, self, and others is the heart of the "Our Father."

One import of this connection for our prayer life is that we pray for others. But the way of our prayer must be distinctively Christian. We do not observe from afar and then pray to a far God to intervene with solace and strength. We compassionately enter the life of another and pray out of the pain and possibility of that life. It seems that one way Jesus bound himself to others was that he prayed *for* them *with* them. With Peter he entered his impetuosity and fear and prayed that Satan not sift him like wheat. With the disciples he entered their temptation to division and prayed that they be one as he and his Father were one. From the cross he understood the ignorance of his executioners and prayed they hear the word of God's forgiveness. Jesus shared the lives he prayed for. We also must "take on" the thoughts and feelings of others, if only vicariously, so that our prayer is not condescendence but our own voice joined to the voices of our brothers and sisters.

Jesus prayed for others through God. He did not enter their lives and pray on their own terms, for often those terms were either self-preoccupation or self-hatred. Nor did Jesus merely push his own agenda, thinking that in the last analysis all people followed the same rhythms that he did. Jesus merged and prayed with other people through the reality they shared in common and the reality that was capable of reconciling them — the love of God. This means that Jesus' prayer for others is not just for anything. His prayer may include many petitions — strength for Peter, unity for his disciples, forgiveness for his enemies — but they are all variations on a single theme. His petitions for others are the same as his prayer for himself. It is the prayer that begins with his baptism, peaks in the garden, and ends in the life of the resurrection: "Whatever else, thy will be done."

THE GOD WHO FELL FROM HEAVEN

XXXXXXXXXXXXXXXXXXXXXXXXXXXX

Only when the last line of all our petitions for ourselves and for others is the furthering of God's Kingdom will the God of Jesus be present.

These religious reflections on prayer are a backdrop to the actual prayers of this volume. Although they are billed as an introduction, they are really a postscript. I found myself praying the words of the following pages and then asked the possible theological basis for them. If the truth be known, I did not so much ask the question as other people pushed me into asking the question. These prayers are companions to those in *The Hour of the Unexpected*. In general there were two reactions to those prayers: (1) "I like them but how are they prayers?" and (2) "I didn't like them and how are they prayers?" This introduction is a hint of an explanation.

These religious reflections on prayer seem to yield three categories into which the various prayers of this volume can be loosely gathered.

Encounters records times when the Mystery clouds or clears our eyes, fills or empties our heart. These incidents differ from person to person and can bring feelings as diverse as wonder and terror. Any time at any place can be an occasion of the outbreak of Mystery. The one prerequisite is that business is not usual. At these times we are beyond the immediate and beneath the surface. We are in the zone of God.

Reflections records times of deepening, times when we make the Christian message our own. We may ask what it means to be thirty-five and holding or how Jesus, the Master of Shock, is also the Good Shepherd or what a real grace before meals would sound like. When we do this reflecting, we personalize the faith we have inherited. We allow it to take root in us and we position ourselves as creatures and believers. Our faith may be encapsulated in single stark statements like "God is love," but its implications burst slowly, like delayed fireworks, over the long days and fast years of our lives.

Connections records prayers for other people, both friends and strangers. Hopefully these prayers are compassionate without being sentimental. Author Flannery O'Connor once remarked that senti-

XXXXXXXXXXXXXXXXXXXXXXXXXXX

ment was giving more tenderness to things than God does. Since in the Christian tradition the presence of God is both judgment and love, our prayers for ourselves and for others must be both affirming and challenging. If all our prayers do is stroke us, we only know a God of strokes. But the God of Jesus is the Lord of transformation or, in the little used metaphor of the Old Testament, a potter; and our unbreakable connection with each other is that together we live under the pressure of those shaping hands.

Although prayer is inevitable for anyone caught between birth and death, it can be marginal to the journey. At its best, prayer is not a way of being pious but a creative way of being human. It is an activity by which we own our days and nights and do not let life happen to us like an accident we are in but in no way caused. In prayer we appropriate the times of strength when power has to be channeled and the times of weakness when power has to be summoned. Prayer brings to mind and heart the identity we cannot escape. It holds together the line from Bernstein's Mass "How easily things get broken!" with the running cripples, seeing blind, and hearing deaf of Jesus' God. In the fifteenth chapter of Luke, three things — a sheep, a coin, and a son — are found. Most importantly, after each finding there is a party. One of Jesus' most persistent images of God and the folks together is festivity. If that is true, in the last analysis the best image of prayer is "music and laughter and good red wine."

Encounters

. . . our love would outlast diamonds

At these times
we are beyond the immediate
and beneath the surface.
We are in the zone of God.

THE GOD WHO FELL FROM HEAVEN

XXXXXXXXXXXXXXXXXXXXXXXXXXXXX

The Prayer of a Grandmother

Knowing she should not overdo it
the way other grandmothers do
she chose between them.
While the salesgirl drummed
long, green nails
on the side of the register,
she rummaged through her purse
wondering aloud where her wallet was.
She counted out careful dollars
for the sunsuit.
But when she arrived at her daughter's door,
the noise of the child inside
so achingly crashed into her silence
she knew
she should have bought
the doll.

JOHN SHEA

A Prayer at Baptism

I must remember, Johnny,
to tell you —
perhaps on some teen day
when your loneliness
is as loud as a rock concert —
how
fresh from the bent space
you came among us
in a new womb of blankets.
You belched and laughed and wailed,
your face as friendly as a dog's tail.
We did rites over you
with all the ceremony of a primitive tribe
painting their babies.
Your grandfather,
his thumb the trunk of a tree
winter could not break,
traced a cross on your forehead
like a man signing a will.
Your parents held you
under a waterfall of grace
and your sleeping eyes
suddenly sat up and stared
into the funny faces of our love.
We made you our own
by making you God's.
Your uncle Len played paparazzo
and has the evidence of all this
in a box somewhere.

THE GOD WHO FELL FROM HEAVEN

XXXXXXXXXXXXXXXXXXXXXXXXXXXXXXX

Afterwards
you slept
and we ate and drank and laughed
and knew
our love would outlast diamonds.

I must remember, Johnny,
to tell you.

JOHN SHEA

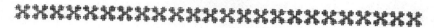

A Prayer for the Fruit Eaters

The old wake before traffic.
From six on the day is theirs
and Joe scrupulously scrapes the toast
and Mary tips the tea
into the saucer to cool
then back to the cup to drink.
The day stretches before them
like a race without a ribbon at the finish.

They are the first at the supermarket.
Their cart seems to move by itself
through the maze of aisles
like a mild horse who knows the route.
It stops in Produce.
Mary squeezes the peaches
and Joe inspects the apples.
By the time the cart reaches frozen foods
a core is shoved deep
into the pocket of his gabardine jacket
and a sticky seed, wrapped in Kleenex,
lies among pennies in the bottom of her purse.

THE GOD WHO FELL FROM HEAVEN

✖✖✖✖✖✖✖✖✖✖✖✖✖✖✖✖✖✖✖✖✖✖✖✖✖

At the checkout
it is: Minute Rice
*   tea*
*   crackers*
*   Jello*
*   cottage cheese*
*   soup.*
She counts out stamps and coupons.
Out of long habit
she pays at the grocery
and he at the gas station.

Outside
the merciless sun hangs motionless
in the morning sky,
although the earth has turned many times.

JOHN SHEA

The Prayer of the Driver

Even at fifty-five
the hitchhiker did not blur.
Sharp, unmistakable muscles
and too much of a smile.
The sign began
beneath his beard.
St. Louis.
I won't
hurt you.
My foot never left the pedal.

✕✕✕✕✕✕✕✕✕✕✕✕✕✕✕✕✕✕✕✕✕✕✕✕✕

The Prayer of Diana at the Beach

The Good Humor man stares
over the sticky coins
the small hands are pushing at him.
The eyes of the vigilant mother
for a moment leave her child.
The businessman on lunch break,
tie undone and suitcoat over the shoulder,
is feasting.

In carefully cut cut-offs
and T-shirt announcing
WILDLIFE,
wading knee deep
in the warming waters of June,
Diana is still.
Her face is flung back,
her eyes closed,
an offering to the sky.
For the moment
the sun is her only lover.

Others are waiting.
She knows it.

The Prayer of a Nine-Year-Old

If you were nine in 1950
and took swimming in the summer
at the Village Day Camp
you were most likely a tadpole
who did not know
he was destined for froghood
but dreamed of sharks
who swim where they will.

The short cut home from camp
was over the thick, knee-high hedge
of Devine's apartment building
and the only shoes
capable of such sustained flight
were black-and-white, ankle-top Ked's Flyers.
The shoe salesman said they fit
but the true test would be
my feet on the air above the hedge.
And I did feel free of the earth
but only the way
a jumping fish hangs for a moment
above the water.

I told my mother
the gyms did not fit.
She said
it was too late
to take them back.
I wore them
like weights.

THE GOD WHO FELL FROM HEAVEN

XXXXXXXXXXXXXXXXXXXXXXXXXXXXX

The next day
adulthood made an unscheduled visit.
As I made for the hedge,
I saw the future
like the look of recognition
in the bulging eyes of a frog.
Hedge flying would wait.
The sidewalks must be mastered.

JOHN SHEA

The Prayer of the Runner

Slowly, my soul,
stretch your stiffness
and uncramp the fetal legs of sleep
with strong kicks off the morning earth.

Easy, my soul,
pace is all
and with pace comes presence.
Do not rush the rhythm.
Groove.

Rise, my soul,
to the mantra of the run.
Listen to the music
the muscles make.

Stride, my soul.
High, my soul.
Ah, my soul,
caught
not from the back
but out in front
where breather and breath
runner and race
are one.

✖✖✖✖✖✖✖✖✖✖✖✖✖✖✖✖✖✖✖✖✖✖✖✖✖✖✖✖✖

A Prayer of Good-Bye

And we came
at last
into a night of rain
where our practiced ploy
of love wrestle
and bed talk,
of sealing a future
before shaping it,
of hope before faith
and love,
like a ceiling
Michelangelo missed,
always
could not keep us
from the glare of day
which never,
as the poet says,
breaks
but handhold by handhold
climbs the east,
the blood of its assent,
spilling into the room
where you are gone.

JOHN SHEA

A Prayer of Communion

On a day
that would not become day,
when fog made the sun a memory
and the unceasing night rain
gave morning a midnight mood,
the car took the forest preserve drive
to become one
with the gray, wet world of woods.

It was already inhabited.
By the side of the road
mounted on a motionless horse
she waited,
the fog hugging her,
the rain braiding her hair,
her jeans and shirt
dripping the low sky.
She blurred and focused
with the swish of the wipers.
As the car splashed past,
her soulful eyes
moved beyond the locked doors
into the dry interior of the driver.
The rearview mirror caught the fog and forest
carrying her away.

THE GOD WHO FELL FROM HEAVEN

XXXXXXXXXXXXXXXXXXXXXXXXXXXXX

Now on days
that will not become day,
she waits
in the downpour of memory,
about to dissolve into earth and sky
but bearing for the moment
the marks of communion.

XXXXXXXXXXXXXXXXXXXXXXXXXXX

A Prayer for Someone Else's Home

*I just happened to be
in my old neighborhood
the way as a teen-ager
I just happened to be
near Mary Alice's house.
The winter sun is never kind
but today it is as unblinking
as a microscope on cancer.*

*Is this the right street?
I cannot smell my mother's waffles.
And the swing
where my father and I sat
and his policeman's hat fell
with laughter over my eyes
is gone.
And the porch
where my grandfather smoked after Mass
and read me the Sunday funnies with a brogue
is too small for the both of us.
And the two flats
are squeezed together
suffocating the gangways
where I raced away my youth.
And the alley
of my duels and daring
is rusted garbage cans
with gashes in the side.*

THE GOD WHO FELL FROM HEAVEN

XXXXXXXXXXXXXXXXXXXXXXXXX

Breaking my reverie
a small boy
with a muffler only a mother could tie
and eyes like Christmas tree lights
runs down the steps of my house
and into a world
which one day
will be taken from him.

A Prayer of Danger

The hubbub of the family party overrode
the clank and sputter of the old air-conditioner
which was stuck in the window
like a block of ice.
The grown-ups with beer were in the kitchen
and the kids with Coke in the den
when Janie lurched into the kitchen.
Her eyes were no longer seven.
Alarm rang her
like a bell that never knew
it was born to be struck.
Her mouth was open
without sound.
From some archetypal jungle
her mother the panther sprang
and slapped her back.
A peppermint popped from her throat,
a sticky pearl on the kitchen floor.
The mother kissed her cub,
and for a moment
there was only
the broken whir of the air-conditioner
circulating the panic in the air
and the mouths of the men
nursing long-neck beers
which for one sweet pull
were milk.

The Prayer of a Swimmer

He had gone out too far.
From shore there was only a form,
the color of flesh,
bobbing into sight
then disappearing in a swell.
We waited,
trading thoughts of terror,
and watching the slow roll
of the blue-green graveyard.
If he had gone under,
our only callous choice
was to return to our gin & tonics
and wait for the ocean
to deliver him to the beach.

When he made the sand bar,
he stood and stared at us
He had only one arm.
A woman called, "You scared us.
You went out too far."
The bright, rolling beauty of the ocean
returned with his smile.

On shore
he ran a towel
across his chest and stump
and looked back at the ocean
like the first man ever to crawl from the sea.
"Nothing to worry about," he said.

XXXXXXXXXXXXXXXXXXXXXXXXXX

A Prayer for Old John the Altar Killer

The Vatican Council decreed:
the priest must face the people.
So the marble once mumbled to,
slammed against the back wall
by the God of sacrifice,
must be dismantled
lest the God of community
be offended.

So the pastor hired old John
who always entered the church stoop-shouldered
expecting the worst from above.
He tarped the area,
masked himself,
told the pastor
he did not know altars grew old
and struck.
Not the rhythmic blows
of proud demolition
but short, panicked punches,
like an alley fight,
his breathing too fast,
his only thought
the street outside.

No lunch.
Done by three.
All the time
his sledge
the weight of dead men.

A Prayer at the Carnival

Every year at St. John's carnival
they pose chubbettes on swings
and put in their five-year-old laps
a squiggly puppy to love to death.
The mothers stoop like umpires
over the shoulders of the photographer
and coax adorability.
But this year
the parents' eyes are infrared,
their heads spin at normal noise,
and they check their children
like a restaurant bill.
They remember
the last night of last year
and how the heat of the day
still shimmered from the asphalt
and the shirtless boy
on whom there was no fat
and the way his molded ribs tensed
when the pistol in his hands bounced
and the irretrievable eyes
of the girl with the stuffed giraffe
who dropped like a vanilla cone
on a summer sidewalk.

XXXXXXXXXXXXXXXXXXXXXXXXXX

Fitzgerald's Prayer

Four doors in
from the corner of Racine and Polk
stands Fitzgerald's two-flat,
undaunted by neighborhood change.
He built it
in the summer of '25
without ever taking
the pipe out of his mouth.
All the time he worked
he saw a cottage by the sea
and felt the spray of salt
in his face.
Two feet before the roof
is a swath of stone
the width of the building
and carved in it a single word
as permanent as the cave at Lascaux

FITZGERALD

The Post Office insisted
he also have a number
but Fitzgerald said
why should he
when any fool could see
that it was his.

Fitzgerald regrets
he can no longer walk to the corner
for a pail of beer.

THE GOD WHO FELL FROM HEAVEN

XXXXXXXXXXXXXXXXXXXXXXXXXX

But at least he has his porch
and with his pipe and rocker
he sits through the seasons
spying on the foreigners.

On Sundays
Fitzgerald's daughter's husband
comes to get him
and takes him to a house
with no name in front
and a stenciled number on the door.
He sits silently on the brick patio
and eats burgers from the Weber.

But on Sunday night
the Ortegas visit his porch
with corn chips and guacamole
and he tells them about
a farm of rocks
in a land of rain
and the peaceful crackle of peat
burning through the night.

✖✖✖✖✖✖✖✖✖✖✖✖✖✖✖✖✖✖✖✖✖✖✖✖✖✖

Reflections

. . . humans need a space beyond hassle
to hang a sanctuary lamp
and consult all there is
about who they are.

Our faith may be encapsulated
in single stark statements
like "God is love,"
but its implications burst slowly,
like delayed fireworks,
over the long days
and fast years of our life.

✗✗✗✗✗✗✗✗✗✗✗✗✗✗✗✗✗✗✗✗✗✗✗✗✗✗✗✗✗✗

A Prayer for Julie's Place

Julie, who is three, has set up house
in her mother's end table.
At cocktail time
a martini sits on her roof
and through the latticework
she can be heard
dazzling her doll
with secrets hidden
from the foundation of the world.
Soon she will outgrow
this sacred space.
Her mother fears the bathroom is next.

But after that — where?
Perhaps
the dark back of a Gothic church
or a clearing in the woods
or a chair which proves the lap of God
or a porch with a presence
or a hill the setting sun plays to
but surely somewhere
for humans need a space beyond hassle
to hang a sanctuary lamp
and consult all there is
about who they are.

XXXXXXXXXXXXXXXXXXXXXXXXXX

A Prayer to the Master of Shock

When you told the seventy-two
to travel without bread and coin,
was it to boggle the mind of the rich
and buckle the heart of the fat?
For you were the master of shock,
dancing out of the desert of fast
with the message in your mouth
that the earth had not yet cooled.
Then you said
the far-flung God was as close
as the widow without justice
and the stranger without a roof.
And you rose up,
like an open hand in a time of war,
and stood by every fire and sea
wherever ear would hear and eye see,
hanging stories like axes in the air
about a son of shame who returns to fanfare
while a son of duty stays without party,
about a worker who bears the heat of the day
while an afternoon stroller is the first played,
about a son who says yes and means no
while another says no and means yes,
about a priest who passes by the other side
while a terrorist wraps wounds,
about a poor man who dines with Abraham
while a rich man cannot find a finger of water,
about a good man whose prayer is swallowed in air
while a sinner has the ear of God.

THE GOD WHO FELL FROM HEAVEN

XXXXXXXXXXXXXXXXXXXXXXXXXXXX

And when the cripple
at the Sheep Pool of the Five Porticos
told you
the water only heals
when the angel troubles it,
you turned on him like a knife,
"I am the water that troubles."

A Prayer for Growing Up at Thirty-Five

I am still looking
for footsteps to follow
like the phony feet
they paste on dancing room floors.
I do not want every day to arrive
like a blank page in a typewriter.
I want the clarity of a slice of moon
and the security of a lottery winner.
My soul yearns
for a turn-of-the-century Eden
with a weekday lunch at home
and jam preserves in mason jars
and naps on the swing
after baseball and beer.
On weekends
I want my mind to click off
like a construction site at night,
I want
routine without monotony,
expectation without pressure,
money without work,
love without need
and if I do not get it,
I will hold my breath
till my face turns
as blue as a circus balloon.

But over my shoulder
a chorus of heaven and earth,
finally finding a ground of agreement,
chants like marchers for a doomed cause,
"Oh grow up!"

The Prayer of Different Types

Lord God,
the never knifed bleed words
and come to you
out of the rush hour traffic
with bumper-to-bumper syllables,
chatting about how their day went,
standing you in the kitchen with a drink
while they putter with supper.

But the ones who fear
holy ground burns shoes
lurk in the shadows of thurible smoke
with some tongueless pain or love,
as silent as Zachary
before the birth of John,
each day rephrasing what they will say
and each night knowing it can only be,
"Blessed be God."

And then there are nomad hearts
camping and decamping in desert storms,
the hope of a milk and honey home
long abandoned.
The cool water of your words,
Lord God,
has turned to the sands of search,
the high romance of pilgrimage
now only the fierce determination
to go on.

A Prayer of Inheritance

I laugh to remember
how
in the second grade
the nun made us slide over
to make room for a guardian angel.
Since I was fat
and the seat thin,
I oozed over the edge
like a melted cheese sandwich
and was painfully aware
of how close God was.
But I have outgrown that angel,
left him behind
like the sign of the cross
before a free throw
in a basketball game.

Yet
if I could tell a son
only one wisdom,
I might whisper
that he had an angel his own,
not as valet
or imaginary playmate,
but as a companion —
like Tobit had
on his mission of manhood.

THE GOD WHO FELL FROM HEAVEN

XXXXXXXXXXXXXXXXXXXXXXXXXXXX

Otherwise
he might forget
his father's mature faith
that the wings of God's love
beat above us all.

I laugh to remember
but I wonder
how to pass on.

A Prayer at Mass

I came to Mass today
to hide in Latin words
and smell the dust of ritual.
I came for sanctuary
where the powerful and poor
together kneel
and unstoppable time
holds still
like a snapshot in the eye of God.
I came to a place without lessons,
where no one is distilling truth
like Tennessee whiskey.
I came to float like a flower
in a Japanese pool.
I came
for the veins under my skin
to swell like the virgins in Nazareth
and burst wine.
I came for something
you cannot get over the counter.
I came because justice
will not happen before cocktails.
I came because my child's cold
did not gather in her chest
like a summer storm.

THE GOD WHO FELL FROM HEAVEN

XXXXXXXXXXXXXXXXXXXXXXXXXX

I came
because in my nightmares chases
I wake to sweat
the moment before capture.
I came
because I want it to be true
that I will go in peace
when this Mass is ended.

The Prayer of a Questioner

Einstein said,
"God does not play dice with the universe"
but to us night-pacers and nail-biters
it sure looks like craps.

Lord of the random,
which is it —
St. Christopher on the dashboard
or Styrofoam dice from the rearview mirror?

Lord of roulette,
you and I have watched
the marble spin before.
You know I become suspicious
when mowed grass
burns brown
in the afternoon heat
and that I part the hairs
you scrupulously count
to catch the real message
sketched in the scalp.

For some
faith is as simple as a clothesline
strung in the backyard sun.
But all the eyes of the edgy see
is a gallows
for shirts and sheets.

THE GOD WHO FELL FROM HEAVEN

�֎✻✻✻✻✻✻✻✻✻✻✻✻✻✻✻✻✻✻✻✻✻✻✻✻✻✻✻✻✻

You know, Lord,
that I will always ask a third time
if you love me
and in the park wonder
if we are not kidding ourselves
when we push laughing children on the swings.

A Prayer of Birth

In the mythic land of the Spirit,
where nothing happens
as a matter of course,
the time had come
and the baby did not.
The midwife rolled her eyes
and bit her beads.
"The child clings in fear.
There is not enough love."

So the father of the child
stood before the misty eyes
and full body of his wife
and seized her hands
like the ropes of a sail.
Then he threw his mind
into his first memory of her.
With a second heave
his heart followed
and steadied his mind
which tended to flit
like a bird over wormless ground.
Then he flung his whole self
into the power of God
which carried him to a time
which could never be again
and it was.

THE GOD WHO FELL FROM HEAVEN

XXXXXXXXXXXXXXXXXXXXXXXXXXXXXX

Now he journeyed a second time
through their days and nights
and all they ever felt
rushed through their interlocked hands
till the child let loose his grip
and was born wailing,
his lungs already bursting with breath.
The lovers laughed
and the child reached for them,
eager to begin.

Grace Before Meals

No formal dress will be required
but you must come
like a child to an ice-cream truck.

Glass-spilling gestures
are preferred
to submissive hands in the lap.
Belching is a compliment to the chef
and pushing peas
on the fork with your thumb
is blessed by God.
But you may not pass the potatoes
unless you come with it;
and if you insist on twisting
a sulking spoon in your soup,
you will be asked for your thoughts
without the pay of a penny.

Now before conversation
there must be silence
or else
why do batons pause
before symphonies begin.

For our subterranean prayers,
the wordless impulses we ride
but cannot speak.

THE GOD WHO FELL FROM HEAVEN

✕✕✕✕✕✕✕✕✕✕✕✕✕✕✕✕✕✕✕✕✕✕✕✕✕

For all who held us once
and now hold us no longer
but who return with upraised glasses
when we hold each other.

For the Lord of the Supper
who eats and drinks with all
and makes marriage wine
so the dance does not die.

Now
by the favor of the festive God,
there is no world but this table,
no time but the moments between us.

A Song of Discipleship
(for the Class of '79)

All things begin in desert sands
where dreams are tempted by demands
and empires rise but fade and fall
before the God who offers all.

We asked the Christ, "Where do you stay?"
He turned and said, "You'll see God's day!"

God lives where dreams chase waking men
and love with laughter catches them;
where people touch beyond the skin
and wingless fly into the wind.

God lives where hope holds out a hand
and healing binds the broken land;
where sun gives sight to blinding night
and peace becomes the just one's fight.

We asked the Christ, "Where do you stay?"
He turned to us and said, "You'll see God's day!"

This Christ we asked now burns us green
and passes on his ancient dream
that we are bound by God's own blood
and fear is swallowed up in love.

His voice still tears the troubled air
with words of mission and of care.
"Your brother thirsts while water flows,
your sister starves and no one knows."

THE GOD WHO FELL FROM HEAVEN

XXXXXXXXXXXXXXXXXXXXXXXXXXX

We asked the Christ, "Where do you stay?"
He turned to us and said, "You'll see God's day!"

Remember, friends, we kiss the earth
and search all things for signs of birth
for God plays drums for dried-out bones
and coaxes shouts from stubborn stones.

So find us near the restful streams
where restless hearts seek out a scheme
to dance with grace down all the days
to honor, glory, and to praise.

A Prayer for Queen Theology

Since theology chases clarity
like a dog after a downed duck,
my praise will be precise.

Theology is skywriting in a Piper Cub,
you cannot blot out the whole heaven
but you can draw a moustache on it.

What I mean is that
tied between birth and death
like Samson between pillars
we push.
What falls on us is theology.

Let me try again by saying that
theology is like cotton candy,
it is not good for you
but what's a Fair without it.

Lest I be misunderstood
theology does not hold the applause meter
for angels discoing on the head of a pin.
It enters the dance.

The truth is,
my wrinkled medieval Queen,
your ageless glory
is that you sleep with the King.

A Prayer to the Good Shepherd

Sheep get sheared. Good Shepherd,
and bleat in their own blood
and so
you did not unlatch the main gate
and scurry the flock
with the long strides of leadership,
making them meekly march
to the jabs of your stick.
Instead
you stole down the sacred mountain
and in the low voice of night
told the stories of God till day.

When the hireling came to the pens
he found them waiting,
straining the sticks for space,
pushing for pasture,
wool in search of wolf.

A Prayer for the Forgotten

Lord God,
memory is as selective as a woman
picking melons at the market.
We arrive at tomorrow
with a bag we ourselves packed.
But what of all
we cannot take with us?
The real wood chair
my father prayed in
left behind when we moved;
the laugh the camera
did not catch;
even times as terrifying
as the teeth of an attack dog.
So much
the Dewey Decimal System
does not catalogue.
So much
of the storyteller's magic
the clear-eyed day forgets.
So much
the earth absorbs
like lost dimes.

THE GOD WHO FELL FROM HEAVEN

✖✖✖✖✖✖✖✖✖✖✖✖✖✖✖✖✖✖✖✖✖✖✖✖✖✖✖✖

Jesus said
you are the God
who sees in secret
and so picks up
even elephantine lapses.
You remember,
not for grudge or accounting,
but because
the beauty of the kaleidoscope
demands all the technicolor pieces.
Despite what the learned and wise say
you are a white-bearded old man
with the mind of an ageless attic
and the heart of a grandmother's kitchen
who stores,
not in the calculated cuts of a computer,
but in the messy way of love
all we are.

XXXXXXXXXXXXXXXXXXXXXXXXXXX

A Prayer for a Penance Service

Seventy times seven God,
we come to confess
that often our lives fall
like smashed tablets to holy ground.
We say we will love
yet we manipulate.
We say we will dialogue
yet we dominate.
We say, "Speak truth!"
yet we hide in lie.
But the frustration of Paul
that the good we would, we do not
and the evil we would not, that we do
yields to the arms of the old man on the hill
who meets the self-hating scripts of the hired hands
with the robes of sonship
and the rings of daughterhood.
You are the father of parties
and no one outruns your joy.

Jesus told us
that for you
it is as easy to say walk
as to say forgive.
Say them both to us,
that we may walk in forgiveness.

A Prayer to the True Man

You often step from the pages
with long, attacking strides,
pushing past fields of the dead
burying their own,
blasting a fig tree
for the simple lack of figs,
followed by men
whose hands never leave the plow.
You are as unyielding
as the desert sun,
Jerusalem in your eyes,
Kingdom in your blood.
You scare me.

Then I see you
in the nights of mountain prayer
over your head with a God
who bargains for more than he gets;
and in the airless garden
with your gasping backdoor plans
and cry against the cup;
and on the lonely wood
with the last and loudest fear
that no one visits the dying.
I know you after all.

Magnificat

All that I am
sings of the God
who brings his life
to birth in me.
My spirit soars
on the wings of my Lord.
He has smiled on me
and the blaze of his smile
no woman or man
shall ever forget.

My God is a gentle strength
who has caught me up
and carried me to greatness.
His love
space cannot hold
nor time age
and all quicken to his touch.

My God is a torrent of justice.
He takes the straight paths
in the minds of the proud
and twists them to labyrinth.
The boot of the oppressor
he pushes aside
and raises the lowly,
whom he loves,
from the ground.

THE GOD WHO FELL FROM HEAVEN

XXXXXXXXXXXXXXXXXXXXXXXXXXXX

With his own hands
he sets a table for the hungry
but the unfeeling rich
suffer the cold eye
of his judgment.

Our mothers and our fathers
he has held in his arms
and the future grows
like this child within me
for the God of whom I sing
bears us his son.

JOHN SHEA

XXXXXXXXXXXXXXXXXXXXXXXXXXXX

A Prayer for Peace

Left alone too long
I am stretched in dream,
a sleepless Samson
struggling between the pillars of night
which do not have the mercy
to collapse,
waiting for the sun
which will not take pity
and come.

Left alone too long
I groove to songs
sung sadly by needles
torturing sounds
from the slow circle of plastic.

Left alone too long
I read away a Sunday sun
and check the mirror for flaws
and leave half the wine
in hope.

Left alone too long
I forget
how your laughter bangs about
my library soul
and your arms carry me away,
like bearers of the pope,
to holy precincts
where peace,
no matter how often knifed,
advances.

xxxxxxxxxxxxxxxxxxxxxxxxxxxxx

A Prayer to the God Who Fell from Heaven

If you had stayed
tightfisted in the sky
and watched us thrash
with all the patience of a pipe smoker,
I would pray
like a golden bullet
aimed at your heart.
But the story says
you cried
and so heavy was the tear
you fell with it to earth
where like a baritone in a bar
it is never time to go home.
So you move among us
twisting every straight line
into Picasso,
stealing kisses from pinched lips,
holding our hand in the dark.
So now when I pray
I sit and turn my mind
like a television knob
till you are there
with your large, open hands
spreading my life before me
like a Sunday tablecloth
and pulling up a chair yourself
for by now
the secret is out.
You are home.

✖✖✖✖✖✖✖✖✖✖✖✖✖✖✖✖✖✖✖✖✖✖✖✖✖✖✖✖✖

Connections

. . . your son
washes the feet of people
who dance in the dust
and calls them not slaves
but friends.

The God of Jesus
is the Lord of transformation
or, in the little-used metaphor
of the Old Testament,
a potter;
and our unbreakable connection
with each other
is that together we live under the pressure
of those shaping hands.

A Prayer for the Nuns of My Youth
(for Dorothy)

It is fashionable now
to burn wimpled effigies,
to picture the sisters of yesteryear
smudging the patent leather finish
on the girls' shoes
and shouting the boys' hands
out of their pockets.
They say
the nuns cupboarded the sexual goodies
and a generation starved.

The bluest nose of all
is not to love
the mix of humanity
that made you.

But I remember
large black dresses of love
who chided and cared
and taught me
to think like an arrow
and feel whatever the air brings
and know that corners are for turning.

If blame there must be,
the real charge must be leveled.
Piece by piece
those sisters
placed heaven in catholic hearts
and it is difficult to forgive
so magnanimous a gift.

XXXXXXXXXXXXXXXXXXXXXXXXXXXXXX

A Marriage Prayer

He said he would never go away
and she said she would always be there
so they got an apartment
with a bedroom set that cost too much
and ate spaghetti and Chianti
with breadsticks and butter.
His sky-the-limit potential
ceilinged at forty
and she got pregnant
a respectable three times.
The best was
when she would park the kids at her mother's
and meet him after work
for drinks and dinner.
They would find out
who they were living with
and then go on as always.
The night of their first daughter's wedding
they wondered about it all
and got weeping drunk.
Once
when they were going to see
her mother in the nursing home,
she knew she loved him
and cried.
He told her not to worry.

THE GOD WHO FELL FROM HEAVEN

✕✕✕✕✕✕✕✕✕✕✕✕✕✕✕✕✕✕✕✕✕✕✕✕✕✕✕✕✕✕

On the dresser in their bedroom
they have photos of their grandchildren
holding hands with Mickey Mouse at Disney World.
They never thought their love a fire
so it did not burn out,
this man who would never go away
and this woman who would always be there.

XXXXXXXXXXXXXXXXXXXXXXXXXXXXXX

A Prayer for a Friend
(for Andy)

Whose wit decreed
that electricity would live
between the fingers of friends
and every second question be
why do people trip
and every first
where did the sky come from?
The same who said
that dreams would chase waking men
and love catch them.

✖✖✖✖✖✖✖✖✖✖✖✖✖✖✖✖✖✖✖✖✖✖✖✖✖✖✖

A Theologian at Prayer

O
(that is the vocative
of a cosmic disclosure)
Thou
who cannot become
an It,
Being in whom
all beings participate,
Absolute Future
who masters every present,
Origin and Destiny
of every concrescing actuality
whose Primordial Nature
cannot change
and whose Consequent Nature
cannot sit still,
Unknowable Mystery
who knows us,
Transcendent Third
in every duo,
please help me get tenure.

JOHN SHEA

A Prayer for a Paranoid

You are right.
Life is your name
whispered in other people's ears.

The lady at the toll booth
was laughing at you,
sucker,
as she pressed the sweaty nickels
into your air-conditioned palm.

The waitress lied.
They were not out of snapper.

Ralph knew you were sunburned
when he backslapped you hello.

The dentist deliberately dropped
the pulled tooth down your throat.

Joan trained the dog
to do that.

Be on the lookout,
eyes over your shoulder,
ears geared to jumping noises.
They are everywhere
and they are out to get you.
And do not turn to God
for, rumor has it,
he is on their side.

THE GOD WHO FELL FROM HEAVEN

XXXXXXXXXXXXXXXXXXXXXXXXX

You are left
with two consolations
few in our culture can claim.
The world is not without a purpose
and you have not been overlooked.

JOHN SHEA

The Prayer of a Job Hunter

Gentlemen,
the resume is incomplete.
There is no space to tell you
I can graffiti dead walls to life
and nurse a drink to soberness.
I can hear the scream
that plays at dream
and catch the morning
before it escapes into day.

The soul
that seeps
from the worn corners
of my wife's eyes
I hold.

But, gentlemen, do not fear
my overqualifications.
Like most
I wake at night to worry
and wonder why
the dawn dislikes me.
I duffel bag my doubts
and am as loyal
as a turkey to Thanksgiving.
I have no words
except when words
are all I have.

THE GOD WHO FELL FROM HEAVEN

✕✕✕✕✕✕✕✕✕✕✕✕✕✕✕✕✕✕✕✕✕✕✕✕✕✕✕

Before you, gentlemen,
is an employable man
who inhales the winter stars
and breathes out crystal shapes
which wait for wine,
who sees the fingers of God
rubbing the backs of the broken,
who kisses the spring earth
for arrivals must be welcomed.

Gentlemen, the curriculum of my vitae
is a pinwheel whipping sparkle
to light one large, black fact.
There is not much that I can do.
Hire me.

The Prayer of the Counselor

After the sweet sleep of the warrior
who knows his god is strongest,
he wakes to break the back of day.
He begins with push-ups and juice,
exercycle and shower,
and a ritual of dress
as precise as a matador's prayers.
No moment the day dare present
goes unmastered. Each event
is dragged into explanation.

Yet when his clients
talk of brick alleys
where truck lights
back them into screams,
he finds the widening circles
of his notebook
turning angular,
sharp, jutting lines
which traitorously sketch a map
to some interior city under siege.

XXXXXXXXXXXXXXXXXXXXXXXXXXXX

A Prayer for Young Couples

Unbundled
they linger outside on winter nights,
getting high in that summer space
where the ice of the air
and the coals of the heart
join.
They wonder at the rest of us
who need houses for warmth.

At restaurants
they squeeze in booths,
tight as Siamese twins,
eating with the unconnected hand.
The older couples,
their hands occupied by a utilitarian fork
and a no-nonsense knife,
smile
like they found an old photograph
in a shoebox.

I have an urge to get close,
to sneak to the edge
of their circle of arms
and offer the only romantic prayer
middle age can muster:
Do not make the heart airless
so the treasure will not fade
or try to refrigerate each day
and save it for old age.

JOHN SHEA

A Prayer at the Coffee Shop

*Although there was not much
she had not done,
she remained as unaffected
as a six-year-old
skipping rope to rhymes.
She liked to meet at coffee shops
and drink Sanka with two creams
and enough sugar for a diabetic coma.*

*Today
she stirs and splashes
and nervously blots
the table with a napkin
and comes at last to John.
Last time it was Paul.
Her tears do not wait for the pillow
but jaggedly crack her make-up
and force her to the washroom
for repairs.*

*Innocence is not lost
in the first fumble with another
but when we give up
and say love will not last.
But she believed in love
the way Jesus believed in God.*

THE GOD WHO FELL FROM HEAVEN

XXXXXXXXXXXXXXXXXXXXXXXXXXXXX

She bounces back
as breezy as a country club hostess.
The tears have passed
like an afternoon shower.
"Tomorrow is another day," she says.
Yes — and hell is runny mascara
and heaven another good time.

A Prayer for the New Enthusiasts

*Chalk me up
as suspicious of spiritual surfers
who miraculously hang ten
and never wipe out.
Pentecost cannot be scheduled
from nine to twelve on Sunday
like a Little League game.
When you took me
to the meeting of the upper room,
I wished I was
in the basement with a beer.
When you prayed, I discussed;
and when the Spirit fell like rain,
I grew an umbrella
out of the middle of my mind.
Tongue-tied to English
and the curse of doublethink
I looked on
like a faithless man
or, worse, a sociologist.
I ended as I began,
a rationalist ripe for ghosting.*

*Now, my friend,
my heart may be hard
but my head is not mush
so when the prophet behind me
began to burble
and the garbled God was in my ears
the only real revelation was:
the Holy Ghost has bad breath.*

THE GOD WHO FELL FROM HEAVEN

✠✠✠✠✠✠✠✠✠✠✠✠✠✠✠✠✠✠✠✠✠✠✠✠✠✠✠✠✠✠✠

A Prayer for a Friend in Depression

My friend,
I watched you at Janice's party.
You stood in the corner,
blank and stricken,
like a preternatural child
who stares too long at dead birds
and does not flinch at slaps.
And I have seen you at the cottage
suspicious of the sunned bodies on the sand
and breaking into sane conversation to ask
if beaches
are not really
deserts by the sea.
What eerie resolve you had once,
dispassionately pricing the future,
but now
the bottom of an endless fall rushes up
and you, the master of somersaults,
are helpless and headlong.

For Isaiah
God was an eagle
who takes its young
high in the blue and brilliant sky
where they solo
on the changing winds.
If one flounders and plummets,
the eagle swoops beneath it
and bears it back to begin again.
May the eagle God
bear you up,
my falling friend.

✕✕✕✕✕✕✕✕✕✕✕✕✕✕✕✕✕✕✕✕✕✕✕✕✕✕✕✕

A Prayer for a Bishop
(for Murph)

Jesus winked
when he dubbed Peter the trampoline
an unbounceable rock;
but also thereby issued
(as the documents say)
the first set of pastoral guidelines
for Bishops.

Never forget
there are things more important
than fishing nets.

Preside like a man
unafraid to sink.

Wherever life is transfigured,
build a tent for it is good.

Beware!
Even the maids in the courtyard know
when your speech betrays you.

Remember
the argument about who is first
takes place on the road to the cross.

Always acknowledge
in the troubled mix of flesh and blood
the Son of the Living God.

THE GOD WHO FELL FROM HEAVEN

Listen
for the Spirit in everyone,
even Cornelius.

Sin with the heart
that swims naked to shore
and not with the mind
that will not be washed.

Run with the young
whenever tombs turn up empty.

Murph,
may your crozier
be as lean as a prophet's staff
and your ring
fit the finger of everyone.

A Prayer for the Uptight

If meditation
is like bailing out a rowboat
swamped by night rains,
then Frank meditates.
Not for God
but to declutter,
"a way of not going under," he says.

The Pope
in Frank's hierarchy of needs
is order.
Every morning he wakes
to beat back chaos
like a god
in a primitive creation myth.
On the subway home from work
he wears ear plugs,
allowing his mind
only the sound of his teeth
grinding the day into fine grain.
Any dance with steps,
he dances.
Anything without,
he sits.

THE GOD WHO FELL FROM HEAVEN

✕✕✕✕✕✕✕✕✕✕✕✕✕✕✕✕✕✕✕✕✕✕✕✕✕✕✕✕✕

His constant complaint
is that Joe's drinking,
Marge's dress, Jack's waistline,
Linda's spaghetti and
his mother's phone calls
are excessive.
He has an electrician's fear
of overload.

That is why his friends
are cheering Joanie on
as she unbuttons his cardigan
and leaves pizza on the couch.
Frank watches her
like a man on the side of a pool
and we pray to the roustabout God
for one good push.

A Prayer for a Funeral Director

His patter is perfect,
his voice as modulated
as Muzak
and his nails buffed and glossy.
In a world of violent interruptions
his list of things to do
assures us
that life is about chores.
He talks of weather and traffic
and pours coffee like medicine.
He knows what to do
with gray gloves turned inside out
and how to invite people
so they won't come.
He is not cold
but far off
like a man behind binoculars.

I wonder if —
when it is over
and the family has gone off to lunch
with all those they love but one —
he drives the now empty limousine
past the unvisited winter graves
and rolls down the windows
so the wind of the highway home
can carry the pain to some other place?

THE GOD WHO FELL FROM HEAVEN

�֍✖✖✖✖✖✖✖✖✖✖✖✖✖✖✖✖✖✖✖✖✖✖✖✖✖✖✖✖

The Prayer of the Gang Who Gathers

Lord of picnics,
summer itself is an invitation
and so we gather,
a band of friends,
bound together
    no doubt by our white-hatted virtue
    no doubt by our high-wire wit
    no doubt by our head-turning looks
but if these should ever fail us
(and when have they not)
we might fall back
on the truth
as unobtrusive as ground:
that we are yours
and that your son
washes the feet of people
who dance in the dust
and calls them not slaves,
but friends.

JOHN SHEA

The Prayer of a Writer

With the shock
of a committed jogger
finding mold in his Adidas
I discovered a small spider
living in my typewriter.
Yesterday
he crawled out
on the "t" key
to sun himself.
I held back
the thumb of death,
not out of mercy
but because the ugliest truth of the Bible
is that we kill what offends us
and this eight-legged presence,
like the God of Jeremiah,
was judgment.

the
HOUR
of the
unexpected

the HOUR of the unexpected

by John Shea

THE THOMAS MORE PRESS
Chicago, Illinois

The Hour of the Unexpected was originally published in
1977 by Argus Communications (Niles, Illinois), a
division of DLM, Inc. (Allen, Texas).

Cover design by Jean Morman Unsworth

ISBN 0-88347-276-7

CONTENTS

The Word That Is There   9

XXXXXXXXXXXXXXXXXXXXXXXXX

to the Prayer
that always rises
when my family and friends
gather

THE HOUR OF THE UNEXPECTED

XXXXXXXXXXXXXXXXXXXXXXXXXXXX

The Word That Is There

First something happens.

A friend dies; a child smiles us into wonder; an old lady refuses to be old; an adolescent finds a way out; a secret weakness is painfully exposed; we are unexpectedly kissed.

First something happens.

A short fall is suddenly without bottom; an expectation is reversed; a comforting self-image is shaken.

First something happens.

At the center of our best effort we discover our worst motive. Our perfect plot fails and their sloppiest plan succeeds. In single-minded pursuit of one goal we blithely achieve the opposite. When all retreat at the sight of the dead, we stay and stare and do not know why. First something happens.

In these moments, and many more, we are thrown back on ourselves. More precisely, we are thrown back into the Mystery we share with one another. These moments trigger an awareness of a More, a Presence, an Encompassing, a Whole within which we come and go. This awareness of an inescapable relatedness to Mystery does not wait for a polite introduction. It bursts unbidden upon our ordinary routine, demands total attention, and insists we dialogue. At these times we may scream or laugh or dance or cry or sing or fall silent. But whatever our response, it is raw prayer, the returning human impulse to the touch of God.

This is how it was for Jesus. The Kingdom of God which he preached came as a gift, suddenly overtaking the weariness of the soul. In farming a barren field a treasure is stumbled upon; a corner is turned and the perfect pearl is for sale; out of nowhere an invitation to the King's party arrives. The advent of God, even when we are looking for it, is always surprise and any encounter with Jesus always holds the unexpected. To the lawyer who wished justification Jesus gave challenge. The rich young man wanted advice and received an unwanted suggestion. Zaccheus merely hoped for a glimpse of a prophet yet dines with his savior. The woman at the well came for casual conversation and went away with self-revelation. With Jesus people seldom got what they asked for. They always got more. We pray out of more, when our emptiness is suddenly brimming, when our ravaged lives are called to greatness, when we crash into limits and recoil.

We pray out of our experiences and the Christian Scriptures. We place our personal stories within the Spirit-created story of Jesus. In this placing, in the interaction of the two stories, the deepest meaning of our lives unfold. We discover ourselves in dialogue with the events generated by Jesus, with the personalities who preceded him in faith (Abraham, Moses, Jeremiah) and those who drew faith directly from him (Peter, Mary, Paul). Like all who encounter the Christian story we are spun around. Old worlds are subverted; new worlds rise from the ruins. We are touched by Love beyond love, aware of life within Life. We are timid people suddenly filled with daring. Every word is prayer.

And so the prayers of this book are stories and images, portraits of the human person entrapped and liberated, frightened and thrilled. They record shattering revelations, uncontrolled hopes, fierce desperations, moments of dance and tears. In all this they resonate with the crazy farmers, persistent widows, cheating accountants, wily servants, forgiving fathers, and uninvited guests of Jesus' parables. They remember the courage of Mary, the betrayal of Peter, the abandonment of Magdalene, the fidelity of God, and the compassion of Christ. At times these prayers directly address God; at other times they do not. Yet all are witnesses to grace, stuttering accounts of the God whose ways are not our ways.

In the end, there is only one justification for these prayers. When God either muscles or smuggles his way into our activities, we know all words are betrayals; yet we speak. At that moment prayer is neither guilt nor task but just the word that is there.

A Prayer of Taking Stock

Lord,
this winter night
I have sharpened myself
like a bookkeeper's pencil
bent over random entries.

This winter night
there will be no balance.
The fragments of memory
will not be pieced into a story.
The days are so themselves
they will not gather into weeks.
Each moment is alien to every other,
a life of blazing fireworks,
beautiful and gone,
extinguished in the black and trackless sky.

This winter night
truth will have its way.
I will remain cluttered
like my desk —
beneath a book I've never read
a year-old phone number
of someone I've forgotten.
It will remain a runaway life
with the reins beyond reach
and the rider's eyes blasted into amazement
by the winds of tomorrow.

A Prayer to Jesus

If you drank with the IRS of your day
and traded laughs with whores
yet took time with the bravado of the young man
and knew the wealth of the widow's mite

If you knew
that each man's righteous vision
is built from the splinters of his brother's eye

If you knew
that only earth and human spit
can cure blindness

If you knew
that sun and rain are without prejudice
and wind blows where it will

If you knew
the fresh flesh of lepers
soon forgets its birth

If you knew
why sepulchers are painted white
and the chalices of filth polished

If you knew
that some men sweat blood
while others sleep

THE HOUR OF THE UNEXPECTED

✖✖✖✖✖✖✖✖✖✖✖✖✖✖✖✖✖✖✖✖✖✖✖✖✖✖✖

then you know

I am both thieves
scrounging for the kingdom
and cursing the cross.

XXXXXXXXXXXXXXXXXXXXXXXXXXXX

A Prayer for Young Men in an Old World

Yesterday
you told me
the clouds carried a New Age.
All was malleable to the tender request,
kisses transformed twisted lips,
flowers grew through snow.

Now
prophecy no longer tears the air,
flames no longer dance
on your young heads.
Time has robbed you of breath
and in the spaces of your panting
whispered its weary wisdom:
dreams are foolishness,
the heart a lie.

Now
the hurt and angry questions
are in your eyes.
"Why did you not the tearless city descend to earth
when we held hands on the boulevard of song?
Why did not the fist open and the bomb bay close
when we played naked in the meadows and the lakes?
Are we left with a chemical Eden
or a patch of monastery to make too much of
or the deadening prospect of
a raise after three months
and the sad memory of youth:
I once saw Christ on a white horse?"

THE HOUR OF THE UNEXPECTED

XXXXXXXXXXXXXXXXXXXXXXXXXXXX

Slumped men,
gibbeted on the intractable heart,
parched by vinegar kisses —
beware surprise.
It is the hour of the unexpected.

✗✗✗✗✗✗✗✗✗✗✗✗✗✗✗✗✗✗✗✗✗✗✗✗✗✗✗

The Last Prayer of Petition Ever
**(written between New York
and Chicago 35,000 feet up)**

*Sigmund Freud has put me wise
that God is merely the me
afraid to face the exploding crash of a 747
from the inside.*

*Also it is common knowledge
that doctors reserve the back wards
for people who daddy God for daily bread.
Of course theologians, always the last to know,
keep asking for little red wagons
while everyone else is buying them at Sears.*

*So
heaven is not stormed by my "gimmes."
I no longer beg God
"to make mine enemies
the footstool under my feet."
I am busy with the upholstering myself.
My prayer life has taken a collegial,
adult, Vatican II-ish turn.
I do not beseech a mercy or beg an intercession
(needless to say importuning is out)
but consult with the Senior Partner
on affairs personal, social, and cosmic.*

THE HOUR OF THE UNEXPECTED

✖✖✖✖✖✖✖✖✖✖✖✖✖✖✖✖✖✖✖✖✖✖✖✖✖✖✖

So it is
I wonder who was addressed
when in the sudden drop of an air pocket
my heart relocated to the space behind my teeth
and someone sitting in my seat screamed,
"O my God, don't let the plane fall!"

A Prayer for Tenderness

The stone throwers gather for judgment
in the immaculate, white-walled office
of the parish rectory.
Their target grips the chair,
her fingernails blanch.

She is young enough
to crack gum and giggle;
old enough
to turn her voice to ice,
her eyes to flint.

Just yesterday
a rabbit died from her blood
proving beyond doubt
she is no longer alone
inside her skin.

For once in her life
she wishes
she was alone.

Her father, who by his own admission
is no fool, does not understand.
Her mother wants to know
how she could do this to her.
Her date who scored
is home doing algebra
but his father assures all
the privilege of the car
will not be Jim's for a long time to come,
a very long time to come.

18

THE HOUR OF THE UNEXPECTED

✕✕✕✕✕✕✕✕✕✕✕✕✕✕✕✕✕✕✕✕✕✕✕✕✕✕✕✕✕✕

The priest scribbles
in the sand.

It is now too much.
Her innocence breaks
and spills down her face.
The righteous
whose virtue cannot comfort
have no chalice
to gather those tears.

She stops, straightens.
In search of tenderness
she moves within herself
in primitive descent
to that warm, wet place
where clings her hated child.

✕✕✕✕✕✕✕✕✕✕✕✕✕✕✕✕✕✕✕✕✕✕✕✕✕✕✕✕

A Prayer at the Barber Shop

*It was a magazine to wait by,
nothing more,
page leafing, picture looking, backgrounding
the mindless talk of the barber shop.
It fell open on my lap
and the exploding nakedness of a young girl
raced down a napalm road toward me.
I tried to look away
but her nightmare eyes held me.
In her screaming mouth was my name.
I wanted to move on to Salem streams
or Marlboro Country or even a Buick
To Believe In but like the hobos in Godot
I said let's go and did not move.
I watched her burn.*

*The next page was a year later.
She had been healed.
All the skin of Viet Nam
had grafted her back to beauty.
She wore a white first communion dress
with a blue bow at the waist
and that reticent smile
which is Oriental forwardness.*

THE HOUR OF THE UNEXPECTED

That photo of a restored yellow girl
with her out-of-sight skin surgically pinched
is the never-ending apology of man to his neighbor.
We kiss and make better
what first we wound and make worse.
But thank God for that resurrection picture.
It keeps me from the growing fear.
If she is carnage,
my most tender moment is cruel,
my achieved world the camouflage of death.

A Prayer for the Lady Who Forgave Us

There is
a long-suffering lady
with thin hands
who stands on the corner
of Delphia and Lawrence
and forgives you.

"You are forgiven,"
she smiles.

The neighborhood is embarrassed.
It is sure
it has done nothing wrong
yet everyday
in a small voice
it is forgiven.

On the way to the Jewel Food Store
housewives pass her
with hard looks
then whisper
in the cereal section.

Stan Dumke asked her
right out
what she was up to
and
she forgave him.

THE HOUR OF THE UNEXPECTED

❋❋❋❋❋❋❋❋❋❋❋❋❋❋❋❋❋❋❋❋❋❋❋❋❋❋❋❋

A group
who care about the neighborhood
agree that if she was old
it would be harmless
or if she was religious
it would be understandable
but as it is . . .
They asked her to move on.

Like all things
with eternal purposes
she stayed.
And she
was informed
upon.

On a most unforgiving day
of snow and slush
while she was reconciling
a reluctant passerby
the State People,
whose business is sanity,
persuaded her into a car.

She is gone.
We are reduced
to forgetting.

A Prayer of Lost Purpose

He slept after dinner now.
In his favorite chair
with his belt loosened.
The paper slid from his lap.
He dozed fitfully for he was afraid
Norman Rockwell would sneak into the den
and paint him.
He would enter Americana
in his marshmallow middle years
stuffed with affluent steak
and toasty with radial heat.
And oh god how he longed after
a cold depression corner
where men stamped their feet
and blasted the night with their breath,
their fists clenched against tomorrow.

XXXXXXXXXXXXXXXXXXXXXXXXXXX

The Prayer of the Older Brother

I dreamed
they never saw me —
but then they never did —
my sweated eyes only a moment lifted
from the stubborn land
to catch the blur of foolish father
his robes clutched up,
rivers washing down his beard,
his sandals lost in run
falling on the runaway,
the inheritance thief,
sniffling back to sonship
the music of welcome in his ears
the fatted calf of forgiveness in his teeth.

I woke
the way rejection wakes,
bypassed and bitter.
The only comfort —
no comfort at all —
there are no older brothers.

A Prayer to the Sleepless God

Better a sleepy god
who dozes while men plot
or a god of graft
paid off in prayers
than this insomniac,
pacing the night sky,
missions smoking in his mind,
two star-blazed eyes raking the earth
where his worshippers wait,
not knights of glory
but broken men
who have found the source of healing.

✖✖✖✖✖✖✖✖✖✖✖✖✖✖✖✖✖✖✖✖✖✖✖✖✖✖✖✖✖

A Prayer of Anger

No hymn of praise today.
No hand-clapping alleluia
for the All-Good God
and his marvelous handiwork.
Lord,
a child has been born bad.
He gangles and twitches and shames
the undiscovered galaxies of your creation.
Why could not the hands that strung the stars
dip into that womb to bless and heal?
Please no voice from Job's Whirlwind
saying how dare I.
I dare.
Yet I know no answer comes
save that tears dry up, skin knits,
and humans love broken things.
But to You who are always making pacts
You have my word on this —
on the final day of fire
after You have stripped me
(if there is breath left)
I will subpoena You to the stand
in the court of human pain.

The Prayer of the Commuter

The latest incarnation
of God is stalled
outside the city walls.
He has been betrayed
into a traffic jam
by the kiss of the urban planner.
His is the reluctantly still point
in a 55 mile-an-hour world.
The expressway,
having had its way with him,
hands him over
to the crucified intersection
where the light
is eternally red.
He is nailed in the left-turn lane.

At home,
behind locked doors,
his wife worries the pot roast
to overdone.
His children wait
amid cold lima beans.
Suddenly
the rushing wind
of a car in the driveway.
The thunderous slam of a door.
And lo!
By divine button the garage door
has been rolled away and the Son of Man
appears on a cloud of exhaust.

THE HOUR OF THE UNEXPECTED

XXXXXXXXXXXXXXXXXXXXXXXXXX

He is as a stranger
and moves past his wife and children
without a word.
He reaches into the refrigerator
and their hearts burn within them
as they recognize him
in the drinking of the beer.

XXXXXXXXXXXXXXXXXXXXXXXXXXX

The Prayer of Belief: A Liturgical Creed

*We believe that where people are gathered together in
love*
> *God is present*
> *and good things happen*
> *and life is full.*

We believe that we are immersed in mystery
> *that our lives are more than they seem*
> *that we belong to each other*
> *and to a universe of great creative energies*
> *whose source and destiny is God.*

We believe that God is after us
> *that he is calling to us*
> *from the depth of human life.*

We believe that God has risked himself
> *and become man in Jesus.*

In and with Jesus we believe that each of us
> *is situated in the love of God*
> *and the pattern of our life*
> *will be the pattern of Jesus —*
> *through death to resurrection.*

We believe that the Spirit of Peace
> *is present with us, the Church,*
> *as we gather to celebrate*
> > *our common existence,*
> > *the resurrection of Jesus,*
> > *and the fidelity of God.*

THE HOUR OF THE UNEXPECTED

XXXXXXXXXXXXXXXXXXXXXXXXXXXXXXX

And most deeply we believe that in our struggle to love
we incarnate God in the world.
And so aware of mystery and wonder,
caught in friendship and laughter
we become speechless before the joy in our hearts
and celebrate the sacredness of life
in the Eucharist.

A Prayer for Sacred Things, Sacred No Longer

The sacred pearl
on the forehead of the goddess
has fallen to mere wealth.
The impenetrable mystery of white light
is bitten, priced, and strung
around blasphemous necks.

The Tree at the Center of the Earth
under which Buddha sat
and on which Jesus hung
has been cut into real wood beams
for the ceiling of the games room.

The many mansions in the Kingdom of the Sky
have been leveled
for the highway of interstellar traffic.

Even man,
once immortal jockey
soul rider of the body,
is now dispensable coefficient.
producer, consumer, casualty.

We are the keepers of the garden
but must our mastery turn everything opaque?
Can nothing be more than it is?
Are we left
with the eucharistic world
ground down to bread
and the horrible boredom of a wine
which refuses its mission of blood?

✖✖✖✖✖✖✖✖✖✖✖✖✖✖✖✖✖✖✖✖✖✖✖✖✖✖✖✖

The Prayer of Marianne Wisneski

The Kingdom of God is like Marianne Wisneski
who is thirty-two years old
and who always hides her left hand
because as her mother said,
"The only gold you'll ever have
will be in your teeth."
To make things worse
every day for lunch
she has rye crisps and a diet Pepsi.
And lately she has taken
to crying in the ladies room.

Yesterday
she was graced
by a more-than-ordinary brushing against
in the elevator.
Albert Scynowicz who works in shipping
said excuse me but he had two tickets
to The Who.
That night
to uninterrupted FM
she curled her legs under her on the couch,
allowed her eyes a mist of hope,
and to her surprise
found in her mouth,
like tax money in a fish,
a prayer.

A Memorial Prayer

His fingers were sausages about to burst
that skittered over the endless tweed of his vest.
His tie-knot was hidden under folds of neck
which terraced to a cavernous mouth and stockade
teeth.
His nose battled for breath and his eyes
were permanently sewn open with delight.
Covering the rest of Jonathan
was a cape and propping it up a cane.
Ted Klasser called him
the fattest fop in history.

On one beer Jonathan traveled to a sun-burnt
Pacific atoll where weight was divinity
and he ruled anemic natives as a god.
On two beers his trunk,
formerly disguised as an arm,
flailed the air, sucked the table for peanuts,
scarfed up a third beer, curled it inward to his mouth,
pachyderm style, and with its downing
a serious Jonathan talked of love.
He wasn't fussy.
Anybody with different but compatible equipment.
"Why can't fat boys and fat girls get together
and compare bulges?"

On the bright beach days of summer
Jonathan would retreat to the "Comfortably Cool" Clark,
remove the arm rest on the outside seat in the tenth row,
and talk to the movie screen.
Once while warning the Panama-suited Sidney
Greenstreet

THE HOUR OF THE UNEXPECTED

XXXXXXXXXXXXXXXXXXXXXXXXXXXX

of Humphrey Bogart's nefarious intentions
he was ushered to the sidewalk.
He vandalized the billboard.
"The Clark theatre is unfair to Sidney Greenstreet
and lookalikes."

Death is worthy of tears and torn hair.
Jonathan's was a pratfall and a banana peel.
A heart attack did not claim him
as his doctor had promised.
He choked on a chicken bone.
At the funeral Ted Klasser said that
everytime he left something on his plate
he would think of Jonathan.
It wasn't a god damn eternal flame
but it was some sort of a memorial.

XXXXXXXXXXXXXXXXXXXXXXXXXX

A Prayer for the Secret Solidarity of the Human Race

The man I did not notice
yesterday died today
and left me alone.

XXXXXXXXXXXXXXXXXXXXXXXXXXXX

A Prayer to the Mad Dollmaker

Lord God,
you are too much like us.
When lonely,
you make mistakes.
When love struck,
you are impetuous.

But it was folly
to fall upon unsuspecting earth,
knead a body of clay
and laying on it,
feet to feet, hands to hands,
breathe passion down its mouth
and wake the eyes to wonder
with tears.
When you put no key in its back
but trusted it to the heat of the heart
and the dimness the mind calls light
we knew, old dollmaker,
that you had gone mad.

Some say
you never guessed
til your love-child came to you
in the beauty of the garden and asked,
"When you die
will all this be mine?"

The Resurrection Prayers of Magdalene, Peter, and Two Youths

Like her friend
she would curse the barren tree
and glory in the lilies of the field.
She lived in noons and midnites,
in those mounting moments of high dance
when blood is wisdom and flesh love.

But now
before the violated cave
on the third day of her tears
she is a black pool of grief
spent upon the earth.

They have taken her dead Jesus,
unoiled and unkissed,
to where desert flies and worms
more quickly work.

She suffers wounds that will not heal
and enters into the pain of God
where lives the gardener
who once exalted in her perfume,
knew the extravagance of her hair,
and now asks her for whom she seeks.

In Peter's dreams
the cock still crowed.
He returned to Galilee
to throw nets into the sea

THE HOUR OF THE UNEXPECTED

XXXXXXXXXXXXXXXXXXXXXXXXXXX

and watch them sink
like memories into darkness.
He did not curse the sun
that rolled down his back
or the wind that drove
the fish beyond his nets.
He only waited for the morning
when the shore mist would lift
and from his boat he would see him.

Then after naked and impetuous swim
with the sea running from his eyes
he would find a cook
    with holes in his hands
    and stooped over dawn coals
who would offer him the Kingdom of God
for breakfast.

On the road that escapes Jerusalem
and winds along the ridge to Emmaus
two disillusioned youths
dragged home their crucified dream.
They had smelled messiah in the air
and rose to that scarred and ancient hope
only to mourn what might have been.
And now a sudden stranger falls upon their loss
with excited words about mustard seeds
and surprises hidden at the heart of death
and that evil must be kissed upon the lips
and that every scream is redeemed for it echoes

in the ear of God and do you not understand
what died upon the cross was fear.
They protested their right to despair but he said,
"My Father's laughter fills the silence of the tomb."
Because they did not understand they offered him food.
And in the breaking of the bread
they knew the imposter for who he was—
the arsonist of the heart.

After the end
comes the conspiracy
of gardeners, cooks, and strangers.

THE HOUR OF THE UNEXPECTED

XXXXXXXXXXXXXXXXXXXXXXXXXXXXX

A Prayer of Discipleship

*Trade blood with me, brother and sister, and conspire
to unravel the wrappings of our lives
to gain the consoling terror of truth.*

*It might be one of those classic dupes
like the Holy Grail or the Fountain of Youth
or a wild charge on some suspicious windmill
beating the air and impersonating truth.*

*But some things must be done
out of folly or pride or sin
to fly into the sun
to stand against the wind.*

*You and I
we sniff like bloodhounds through the forest of our lives
to catch a scent of where Meaning paused,
breathless and heaving from our pursuit,
then plunged again into the thicket
where we lost him and our youth.
And in those thickets our middle years will snag
until down a final and forgotten trail
where at last Meaning will be met
he will suddenly turn to greet us
with the bony hand of death.*

*But, brother, we both dimly see
    the struggle is the goal
    the search is what we know.
All the rest is heaven.*

JOHN SHEA

XXXXXXXXXXXXXXXXXXXXXXXXXX

Then
when despair was ripe and bursting
the hand of a laughing angel
pushed me over the edge of Sunday afternoon.
Down the screaming cliffside of my soul
I scraped for a handhold.
The black beach rushed upward.

There
on that black beach
in the everlasting night
I let loose the choking grip I had on life
and the thieving sea swirled round me
and escaped down the sand
with all I ever held in my hand.

Now of a sudden, of a sudden
in this moment of my breaking
came the absurd dawn of hope
and embryonic God began his growth.

So arbitrary, so crazy
like shooting dice for apostleship
or listening for the spirit in the wind.
Like some mythic Greek, astride the stars,
from an ornate urn slung on his shoulder
had poured a terrible beauty
over the earth.

THE HOUR OF THE UNEXPECTED

And so, brother, in this runaway comedy
we bungle through
a pilgrim is stretched across the sky
and I will cast my lot with him
    for fellowship and more
he is a man like me
        and more
    who will scream the absence of his God
            and die
        then leave behind some Palestinian knoll
            at dawn
                a broken tomb.

XXXXXXXXXXXXXXXXXXXXXXXXXXXX

A Prayer at Burger King

He was accustomed to making women laugh
and saying blushing things
which forced them to stare downward
into cups of coffee they never saw.
So when Alice called the third time
and knowing how hard it is
for heavy girls to get a date,
he suggested lunch at Burger King.
He wore his blue blazer and white turtle neck
which made it clear to all
that Whoppers were not a habit
but the slumming quirk
of a man used to better.
He gave Alice a quick progress report
on his miraculous rise at Zenith.
She was into God
and told him he was empty
at the center.
Jesus could stuff his hollowness
and he could lean on her
in his misery.
After that
he did not answer her letters
and when she phoned
he suddenly discovered guests.
But he spent time at the mirror
wondering
if his winning smile
was really fiercely gnashed teeth
and his hard, clear eyes
the site of future weeping.

A Prayer of Unwarranted Hope

Lord,
if I believe that Satan,
as St. Peter says,
roams about seeking whom he may devour;
I would say
he had made a meal of her.
All her words were ugly:
all her thoughts were schemes.
She took revenge
on anyone
with judgment poor enough
to love her.
Her only tears
were icicles of spite
and she slapped away
the hands of help.

Now
she tells me
the demon has moved out.
She is a house swept clean,
a space of pirouetting light.
And I am caught
once again
in the embarrassment of hope
which this time did not have the good manners
to merely glimmer
but the beautiful rudeness
to burst.

JOHN SHEA

A Prayer to the Ever-Enticing God

I am embarrassed for you, God.
A promising paradisiacal beginning
that fizzled, nothing to show
but some murdered messengers
and a crucified son rescued three days
after the nick of time.
And recently you have tripped
into the credibility gap.
You are a joke in academia,
the household pet of rectories,
and everyone is saying you have to be rethought.

And now look at you,
acting out for attention.
A lampshade on your head,
making faces for laughs,
insisting Paul said party always
not pray.
And now you come to me
with a fiddle and a jug
and the grasshopper notion
to entice my ant-like industry,
to strike a tune and dance off with you
into the long winter.
Are you kidding?
Let's go.

A Prayer of Death

On retrospect
it was more than an unwilling contraction
and a pelvic push,
more than the spine knitting
and the synapses wiring
in those nine months.
Courage was making a small fist
in the dark warmth.
A glaring passage of light
promised me the world
and I trusted it.

Now
they wait around my bed
with cups of hospital coffee.
The doctor says I've slipped
but I have only clenched the sheet
because an unmoored sun wants to warm me.
The glaring passage of light has returned.

Two Prayers of Loss

I.
Thaddeus Edward Bornowski
would not be at the lathe today.
It was the 24th of June
and he was angling his kitchen chair
down the narrow back stairs.
It slid perfectly into the trunk
of his car. It had been there before.

It was seventeen minutes to St. Adelbert's
and three winding, five mile-an-hour minutes
to the Holy Rosary section
and just a moment past
the stone bead of the Annunciation
to Rosemary Dorothy Bornowski
*   1909-1968*

He set the chair on the side,
leaned over with kitchen intimacy,
and talked downward
past the plaque and grass,
the settled dirt, cement casement,
and the copper casket with the crucified God
to the listening memory within.

THE HOUR OF THE UNEXPECTED

✖✖✖✖✖✖✖✖✖✖✖✖✖✖✖✖✖✖✖✖✖✖✖✖✖✖✖✖

II.
For Daniel and Mary O'Malley
after supper came the beads.
He would Hail Mary the first part:
she would Holy Mary him back
*   and the rote prayer rose to chant,*
*   word ran upon word, a marriage sound,*
*   the Catholic trick for ecstasy.*
Every evening for forty-seven years.

Now she was gone.
The family agreed their father
had held up well
but every night after supper
in the den of his daughter's house
he would Hail Mary
and wait.

XXXXXXXXXXXXXXXXXXXXXXXX

The Prayer of Someone
Who Has Been There Before

After the last time—
*   when I finally turned from flight*
*   and from somewhere came the strength*
*   to go back—*
I rummaged the ruins,
*   a refugee picking through bombed belongings*
*   for what surely was destroyed*
and began again.
*   I grew my new life*
*   thick and rough*
*   with an alarm system on the heart*
*   and an escape hatch in the head.*
It was as spontaneous
as a military campaign.
*   I loved in small amounts*
*   like a sick man sipping whiskey.*
Each day was lived within its limits.
Each moment swallowed quickly.
*   It was not all — our embracement of life*
*   but neither was it the hunched*
*   and jabbing stance of the boxer.*
There was courtesy and a sort-of caring.
*   It was not bad.*

THE HOUR OF THE UNEXPECTED

✠✠✠✠✠✠✠✠✠✠✠✠✠✠✠✠✠✠✠✠✠✠✠✠✠✠✠✠

Now this.
This thing   This feeling
*   this unbidden intrusion*
*   which had no part to play*
*   but played it anyway.*

All those things scrupulously screened out
want in.
*   And I can sense it coming,*
*   a second coming,*
*   a second shattering.*
*   Someone   Something*
*   is at me once more,*
*   mocking my defenses,*
*   wrenching my soul.*
*   God damn it!*
Is it you again, Lord?

XXXXXXXXXXXXXXXXXXXXXXXXXXXX

A Prayer for an Old Lady Ever Young

"Peace to all who dwell in this house."
The priest stamps snow on the hall rug.
"And a good morning to you, Mrs. Kurleen."
Hannah is pillowed round,
wedged into uprightness,
before the morning game shows.
A dark red lipstick is almost on her lips
and the beauty parlor has recently
strategically deployed her thinning hair.
"Hello, young man."
Click. Magic waves
knock the telly into unconsciousness.
"I want to go to confession first."
She winked
promising more
than ordinary fare
and launched in.
"I had some impure thoughts
     but I suppose you never had any of those —
          being a priest."
"Only when I'm around you, Hannah."
"I yelled at my daughter ten times."
"Only ten."
     She hits the priest on the shoulder
     and laughs.
"You don't get any good sins when you're old."
"For your penance
tell your daughter
you are a crotchety old lady."
"No."

THE HOUR OF THE UNEXPECTED

XXXXXXXXXXXXXXXXXXXXXXXXX

"Tell her you are sorry for being bitchy."
"No."
"Blame it on your arthritis."
"Alright."
Hannah smooths her lap
and wheedles.
    "Is it true about Mrs. Mallory's daughter Meg?"
"How would I know?"
    "Ah! I see it is."

"I hear this Altar & Rosary . . ."
but a round, white Jesus,
rescuer of priests,
rises before her eyes
slips between her lips,
and manages
by the sheer breadness of him
to stop the conversation.
Water eases the host down
and Hannah leaves
wet, smeared, red lip prints
on the glass.
Suddenly she is old.

The priest packs up.
"Merry Christmas, Hannah."
"Merry Christmas, Father."

✕✕✕✕✕✕✕✕✕✕✕✕✕✕✕✕✕✕✕✕✕✕✕✕✕✕

The snow of his entrance
is now a dark, wet slash.
It will soon disappear
into the rug.

"Hannah,
your hair-do
is so wickedly attractive
that it's a proximate occasion of sin."

"Thank you, young man,"
she laughs and buttons
the T.V. back to life.

XXXXXXXXXXXXXXXXXXXXXXXXXX

A Prayer the World Cannot Take from You

Like an obedient cat
the purse sat
on her lap.
Her fingers slowly traced
the creases on her forehead.
Her eyes were closed
against the worries
of the waiting room.

Without warning
her lower lip gave way.
A string of dribble
fell to the collar
of her coat.
A sudden handkerchief appeared.
She had old people's ankles.

Out of the inner office
past the smile of the nurse
he stepped
buttoning a gray sweater.
Skin gathered in mounds
on the back of his hands.
He wrestled with a coat
that fit him once.
Her eyes opened. He took her hand.
"Let's go."
"Yes."
and he led her into the dark, December afternoon.

Sharon's Christmas Prayer

She was five,
sure of the facts,
and recited them
with slow solemnity,
convinced every word
was revelation.
She said
they were so poor
they had only peanut butter and jelly sandwiches
to eat
and they went a long way from home
without getting lost. The lady rode
a donkey, the man walked, and the baby
was inside the lady.
They had to stay in a stable
with an ox and an ass (hee-hee)
but the Three Rich Men found them
because a star lited the roof,
Shepherds came and you could
pet the sheep but not feed them.
Then the baby was borned.
And do you know who he was?
Her quarter eyes inflated
to silver dollars.
The baby was God.
And she jumped in the air,
whirled round, dove into the sofa,
and buried her head under the cushion
which is the only proper response
to the Good News of the Incarnation.

THE HOUR OF THE UNEXPECTED

✖✖✖✖✖✖✖✖✖✖✖✖✖✖✖✖✖✖✖✖✖✖✖✖✖✖✖✖✖✖

A Prayer to the God
Who Will Not Go Away

Lord,
you are the poetry of wordless lives,
the salting of tasteless purposes,
the reminder that we are more than
the sinking spiral of the dying sparrow
and that the reckless rush of the galaxies
marvel at the human collision of a kiss.
You are the tightening hope
that someone has stretched a net
beneath this high wire act of ours.

JOHN SHEA

Prayer at Genesareth — Mark 5, 1-20

Holed up within me,
his eyes bleeding
in the crouched darkness,
is a frightened, cellar creature,
the stunted, mongoloid me.

He lurks in guarded depths.
My fear is vigilant.
By day
I overtalk his cries
and if at night he howls
I shut my soul
and play at sleep.

Then Jesus
pushed off course
by a meddlesome squall
crashed on my shore.
With the first syllable
of his unwanted words
like a sudden pregnancy

he stirs.
Even prayer and fasting
are now helpless against
the force of his
delivery.

THE HOUR OF THE UNEXPECTED

He rips.
Bolts.
Out of the mouth of my screams
down the cheeks of my tears.
In the nakedness of his exorcism
his deranged features betray
the practiced sanity of his keeper.

There is no hospitable pig
for easy habitation
or a death-dealing cliff
to bring him rest.
The poor bastard is loose
and he is mine.

I will search him out
among the pliable words of pity
and the delighted face of shock.
I will fall on him with kisses,
swallow him down,
and await our redemption.

JOHN SHEA

An Easter Prayer

Lord of Easter
the words of death . . .
nodule . . . malignant . . . metastasized
are boiled killingly clean,
passed on by forceps.
None of the slop of life is on them.
They do not well up and spill over
or sadly sparkle or break
into syllables of laughter.
They are under orders
to dispatch without recourse.
Begging will not move
these unyielding words of stone
which only you roll back,
Lord of Easter.

The Prayer of the Holy Sacrifice of the Mass

Those who do not believe in a Higher Harmony
will balk when told an accident crunched
in the parking lot at the very moment
the altar boy's nose began to bleed.
He bled on the surplice, the cassock,
the candle, the other altar boy,
and the priest's unlaced shoe
which bulgingly carried an Ace bandaged ankle.
The priest was stuffing a purificator up the boy's nose,
damning the blood into his eyeballs,
when the lector asked, "how do you pronounce
E-l-i-s-h-a" and the organist pounded
the entrance "Praise to the Lord."

They processed.
The bleeding, the halt, and the mute
unto the altar of God.

Saturday was late and liquored
and delivered God's people,
sunglassed and slumping, to the epilogue
of weekend life, the Gothic Church.
They were not the community of liberal theology
nor the scrubbed inhabitants of filmstrips.
They were one endless face
and that face was asleep.

"May the grace of our Lord . . ."

A hungry pause for repentance.
A quick feast of sins.

JOHN SHEA

✗✗✗✗✗✗✗✗✗✗✗✗✗✗✗✗✗✗✗✗✗✗✗✗✗✗✗✗

The lector murdered the prophets once again
and bypassed the section where a certain E-l-i-s-h-a
was having prophetic truck with a widow.
The homily parlayed a fairly clear gospel
(you are either with me or against me)
into sentences of vacillation
and paragraphs of double-think.
The priest ran to the Creed for refuge
only to find a special creed was prepared
for this morning's liturgy by Mrs. Zardek
"I believe in butterflies and the breath of . . ."

The courage of the president
of the liturgical assembly
drained into the bolt holes
of communion rail days.

The offertory gifts never made it.
They were dropped by an elderly couple
("We never liked the new Mass anyway.")
who collided with a small but speedy child
whose highheeled mother was in klicky-klack pursuit
and whose name was "Rodgercomeback."

The consecration was consistent.
The priest lifted the host
and said, "This is my blood."
Instantly aware of his eucharistic goof
but also momentarily in the grip of a bizarre logic
he changed the wine into Jesus' body.

THE HOUR OF THE UNEXPECTED

XXXXXXXXXXXXXXXXXXXXXXXXXX

Then
with his whole mind, heart, and soul
he genuflected
— never to rise —
to a mystery which masks itself
as mistake
and a power which perfects itself
in weakness.

JOHN SHEA

The Advent Prayer

What will come
when all the days
have run upon the nights
and all men climb the tree of Zaccheus
and stretch necks beyond giraffes
to be the first to be blazed
by a star?

We are badly in need of ecstasy.
We freeze in sun and fever in shadows.
We die
amid the flowers of the mind.

Someone
must come to us from the future
prodigally
with rings and robes and kisses
and fall upon our self-reproach
with the tears of welcome.

The star-child is turning
in the womb of the virgin.
We dwell in readiness.
Override the babble of our words
with the raw cries of new life.

Be born, stubborn child.
We wait.

THE HOUR OF THE UNEXPECTED

XXXXXXXXXXXXXXXXXXXXXXXXXXX

A Prayer for New Music

Jesus said
we play dirges and do not mourn,
frantic rock and do not freak out.
A new music must be heard
which will drive us to dance
in a world wrung into flatness.
Tonight will we not all sleep
    with one ear in dream
and one alert
        for the crackling of concrete
        and the blossoming of earth?

A Priestly Prayer St. John
Would Not Approve Of

As usual
I come beaten —
a romantic who knows better
but cannot stop,
a wound down dervish,
his schemes done in by grace,
his glorious quest after the brightest star of winter
ending in a very bad cold.

My priesthood has not lacked causes.
I have marched for peace, picketed for grapes,
sensitized my psyche at Bethel,
gave up sure-fire advice for the Rogerian mirror
(from which now leers the militant Carkhuff)
but I cannot run off to hula hoop salvation,
"putting on Christ" with my Jesus sweatshirt.
I know the exact time of the Second Coming
can only be told on a Mickey Mouse watch.

Ghosts of priests past rise up:
some sons of Eli, the temple gang,
others struggling prismatics refracting
the unapproachable light of God
onto the technicolor earth.
They bequeath both bread and stones,
fishes and serpents.
Yet gifts are gifts.

THE HOUR OF THE UNEXPECTED

XXXXXXXXXXXXXXXXXXXXXXXXXX

They gamble — not without regret —
and wonder if people who look back
really turn to salt.
And in the fidelity of their doubt
they call me back,
their brother in a foreign land,
to my pact of blood with You.

I must return to the Listening Place
to be healed beyond forgetting,
to celebrate without ego tripping,
to find a meaning which is not the best told lie.
I must remember the scatological faith
that You once sneaked off to the woods with the world
and we are the slow gestation of Christ.
In You the most tired truth will be fresh
and I will surrender to victory and find a peace
which is the limitless source of fight.

A Prayer to the God
Who Warms Old Bones

Locked arm in arm,
the wool of winter still around them,
three old women hobble
across the young grass of June.
They have staged a geriatric escape
from St. Andrew's Old People's Home
but varicose veins have forced them
to rest on the bench outside my window.
They settle down for an afternoon
of people watching.
No one can resist.
The boy with the baseball mitt says hi.
The truck driver waves. The mailman
asks how the girls are today.
They giggle and think him silly.
The ladies on the bench believe life
is friendly and when it is not,
they scold it
like a child who must be told he is good.
Yet they wait
(and so do we)
for a passerby, an afternoon visitor,
perhaps that woman
with the baby in the stroller
to tell them the good news —
they do not need coats in summer.

THE HOUR OF THE UNEXPECTED

�֍✖✖✖✖✖✖✖✖✖✖✖✖✖✖✖✖✖✖✖✖✖✖✖✖✖✖✖✖

A Prayer of Amendment

The purgatorial sauna runs last night's bourbon
to the boards and the ditty which inspired
the dawn cab home moans over electric rocks.
Stretched on the hot slates of regret
a modest towel protects the rights
of private perspiration.
The dry heat works a chemical metanoia
on the soggy soul and the dissolute fun
of the old man sweats into the constancy of the new.
Under a shower of ice,
an oath of repentance,
a firm purpose of amendment,

and close upon it

like a self-evident truth
or an inalienable right
in the instant of recovery
the profligacy of the imagination
draws another beer.

A Prayer to the God Beyond God

Architect, Body-Moulder, Breath-Giver
Mountain-Thunderer, Goatherd,
Sky-Dweller, Dream Stalker,
Freedom-Fighter, Desert Shiek,
Bridegroom, Wine-Grower, Potter,
Law-Giver, King-Breaker, Jealous Husband
Judge, Ruler, Priest
Father
Flame, Wind, Gentle Voice,
Grave-Robber, Spirit-Giver
Islam knows you
as the joy
that can only go
ah

✕✕✕✕✕✕✕✕✕✕✕✕✕✕✕✕✕✕✕✕✕✕✕✕✕✕✕✕✕✕

A Prayer of Wholehearted Commitment

Lord,
You have the biblical reputation
of taking people places
they never wanted to go.
Witness Jonah
delivered by whale to Nineveh
and Habakkuk
flown by angel to Babylon.
Also I have heard
You do not consult,
Abraham is suddenly ordered from Haran
and Moses called out of retirement
for the Egyptian assignment,
Furthermore
Paul says
You take a chiropodist's delight
in Achilles heels,
spurn eloquence for the stutter,
and reveal yourself
in the thorns of the flesh.
And what was this unpleasantness
with your Son shortly before
his appointment at the Right Hand?
So it is that to You
my most resounding "yes"
is a "maybe"
and it is with one eye on the door
that I say
"Behold, Lord, your servant waiteth!"

A Prayer of Abandonment

We know ourselves
by the ghosts we fight
    the apparitions of a sleepless night
whom we blast in rage,
treat to cold steel speeches of resolve,
and confide lusts that will not bear the day.
So where were you last night, my good time deity;
    drinking buddy, frat brother
when failure was in my throat
and every word a scream for peace.

THE HOUR OF THE UNEXPECTED

A Prayer to the God of Surprises

Attack
when the sun has turned the lake to flame
and the waves are music on the beach.
Ambush me
in the quiet beyond words
I have with her.
Spring at me
from the running boy.
Vanquish me
in the courage of the weak.
Take me by surprise
in the wrinkled smile
of the lady with the floppy hat.
But be warned.
I will be on my guard
welcoming defeat.

JOHN SHEA

XXXXXXXXXXXXXXXXXXXXXXXXXXX

A Prayer to the Awesome God

I have seen the kingdom children
ark dancing in the temple,
psalming and cymboling,
coaxing grace with a parade of summersaults,
turning your fierce lightening
into sparklers of joy.
They are the lap sitters, the ear whisperers,
tracing a smile on your lips
with the child's confidence
that your heart is laughter.

Forgive
my bowed and kneeling distance
and my Old Testament stutter
when I remember
that the outspread wings of eagles
cover you
and your face is death.

XXXXXXXXXXXXXXXXXXXXXXXXXXXXXXX

Prayer for a Nun in a Wheelchair

In the Convent of Perpetual Adoration
on an eternal summer afternoon
the three o'clock chimes called back
the flight of the old nun.
In her wheelchair
before the God who lives in bread
and runs the risk of staleness
she watched the hour
that Peter, James, and John did not.
Two young ones come for her
with the precise steps of piety
and perpendicular genuflections.
The guard is changed.
She is pushed from the adoration space
but the bright white God goes with her
in the monstrance behind her dimming eyes.
The sacred has performed its slow alchemy.
The wheelchair hypnotically clacks
the revolutions of her exit.
She is maneuvered by the sister on duty
to a sparse clean room with a crucifix and flowers
and placed in the windowed light
where she dwells with silence
and the memory of praise and
the dancing particles of the undying sun.

JOHN SHEA

The Last Prayer of the Man
Who Cannot Pray

The sun which Ecclesiastes says always rises
streaked across the water, lit the shore
like a stage and forced the lone man
to shade his eyes against the overbearing day.
Shoeless, hatless, slacks rolled knee high,
a limp half-opened shirt, a pale sculpting
the night left upon the beach.
Spent white caps foam about his feet
and slip like desperate handholds
back to sea. Sand grips his toes,
sucks tight his heel, cements his arch.
He eases loose. Two perfect prints.
A wave rushes the beach, spreads and runs
upon the prints, blurring, erasing.
Another comes, washing away, smoothing.

The lone man pushes into the sea.
Darkness swirls about his waist,
splashes his chest. He cuts the water
with strong, sure strokes. His kicks
send up a spray. A majestic wave
towers above him.

❇❇❇❇❇❇❇❇❇❇❇❇❇❇❇❇❇❇❇❇❇❇❇❇❇❇❇

A Prayer to the Pain of Jesus

Father,
when crutches were thrown away
did your Son limp
after the running cripples?

Did Jesus' eyes dim
when Bartimaeus saw?

Did life ebb in him
when it flowed in Lazarus?

When lepers leapt in new flesh
did scales appear
on the back of his hand?

The gospels say
Jesus felt the power go out from him
but neglect to say
whether at that moment
pain came in.

Did the Son of God
take on ungrown legs and dead eyes
in the terrifying knowledge
that pain does not go away,
only moves on?

XXXXXXXXXXXXXXXXXXXXXXXXXX

A Prayer for the Long Haul

Allow me not, Lord of Blood,
to be one with the One
and mountaintop smile
on the trashing plain.
Allow me not, Lord of Bone,
to drive out of ambition with a whip of dreams
and smuggle heaven onto the troubled earth.
Allow me not, Lord of Flesh,
escape ecstasy, the inner endless journey,
the noiseless perfections of the soul.
Give me, Broken Lord, the long courage
for compromised truths, small justices,
partial peaces.
Keep my soul in my teeth, hold me in hope,
and teach me to fight
the way farmers with hoes defeat armies
and rolled up manuscripts survive wars.

THE HOUR OF THE UNEXPECTED

❌❌❌❌❌❌❌❌❌❌❌❌❌❌❌❌❌❌❌❌❌❌❌

A Prayer for Baptism

Lord Jesus,
to the disciples' bewilderment
you said,
"Let the little children come unto me."
And so now we gather
     parents, relatives, friends
in the name of this child
     who cannot yet run to you
and ask
that you come to her.
We suspect that in your Father's plan
babies are sent to disarm us.
Our shields are useless
against their simplicity.
May this child as she grows
in age, wisdom, and grace
ever remain the bringer of your peace,
Lord Jesus.

JOHN SHEA

A Prayer of Christmas Past

What boy pulled his stocking cap over his ears
(his unmessable crew cut beneath)
and found the predawn Christmas snow
waiting for him?

The street lights were city stars
guiding magi through the supernatural night.
The boy's holy ambition was to walk the snow
without leaving tracks,
to know everything it was
yet leave it unmarked.
He failed wonderfully
across Romaine's white lawn.
Two blocks away
the bright Gothic God
invited him into the magic darkness
where wars were bells
and nose was pine and incense
and eyes were poinsettias and golden chalices.
As was his host's custom
he surprised him,
like a gift under the tree,
and took him up past the stained glass saints
to the vaulted, wood-carved heaven.
He told the boy he would not fall
then dropped him into Christmas.

What man now strikes the flingy past
to fire the coldness of his soul?

A Prayer to the God Who Lives in Children (for Liam)

*Two foot, two year confluence of bone
and love and blood with bathing suit
slung on roguish hips, hair
that blonds the beach, in primitive pact
with air and sea, sent from
All There Is to blandish sated eyes*

when was it

*in your bowlegged pursuit
to love wrestle the fleeing cat
or when your pinball face
hits jackpot over a soggy chip
chanced upon in the lawn
or in your mercurial, non-nap hours
when drunken, prodigal smiles
are drowned by waterfall eyes*

when was it

*predator of weary adults,
with what burst or flash
or the throwaway grace
of a Charlie Chaplin fall
did you become
the sacrament of God?*

JOHN SHEA

A Prayer for the Church

*Not alone
the passage through the knives and kisses
but you and me and her
and that one with the running eyes
and the man with the incision in his side
and the lady in the size sixteen petite,
a band which camps around the last of light
and tells the story of the broken Son
about the fusion of all men's wrists
and the single eye of God
and tomorrow's march
toward the breaking greyness of the sky.*

The Prayer of Isaac's Birth

The angel said
the withered shall conceive
and Sarah laughed
at the thought of a geriatric egg
wheelchairing down a fallopian tube
to rendezvous with Abraham's exhausted thrust
wheezing and crutching its way toward
collision
which is the sidesplitting hello
of the bar of soap, the cream pie,
the banana peel, the bombing bird,
all things beyond prediction
which loose logic's hold
on the Laurel and Hardy world.

And now you burst in,
pulling back the drapes of a sunless life,
singing off-key enough to wake the dead.
I had forgotten
that for the friends of the storyteller
the impossible is ever happening.
Confinements crack, the caves of permanence
give up their guests
for from the mouth of the resurrected Christ
comes the laughter of Isaac's birth.

JOHN SHEA

A Prayer to Mary at the Cross

On the hill outside the walls
beneath the brutalized memory of New Person
reels the struggled magnification of the Lord.

Woman,
the dead rain falls
and the earth grows cold
and your son no longer
swallows the sky.
But a song of hope
must be struck upon the strings
about fallen sparrows and counted hairs,
the painful prayer of that widow with her mite,
the prophetic fierceness of the sun,
the fire of the desert stars
under which rings the adamantine No of Jesus
to the promises of the Prince
and the everlasting echo in your womb —
Fear not: God stirs.